the
enlightened
gambler

the enlightened gambler

**The heart and spirit
of the risk taker
in all of us**

by
Marty Klein

Cover Art by Charlotte Tusch Scherer
Cover Typography by Maxine Davidowitz

The Enlightened Gambler available for order through Ingram Press Catalogues

Visit my website at www.theenlightenedgambler.com
Printed in the United States of America
Marty Klein Publishing
Woodstock, New York

First Printing: November 2013
by
Sojourn Publishing, LLC.

ISBN 978-1-62747-033-9
Ebook ISBN 978-1-62747-034-6
· LCN Pending

To my well meaning father, Harry Klein, my most cherished mentor, Charlie Kreiner and to my awesome and inspiring stepson, Jory Serota.

THANKS

Charlotte Tusch (Scherer) for being my best friend, my partner, my lover, my confidante and the most supportive ally I have ever had.

Tom Bird Publishers and Rama for being my patient and supportive guides through the crazy and overwhelming new world of publishing.

Steve Davidowitz for his encouragement as he cheered me on with the writing of the book and his assistance with the chapter layout of The Enlightened Gambler.

And last but not least, to all the friends who came in and out of my life throughout the years as comrades and accomplices in the wild world of sports and gambling. We totally immersed ourselves in playing and loving the game over many years and we sure did it brilliantly!

CONTENTS

INTRODUCTION

"...We, the people of the United States, have an endless capacity for taking risks..."
President Obama, excerpts from his January 21, 2013 inauguration speech.

I'm hanging out on the beach in Atlantic City one spring afternoon with my partner, Charlotte. It's gorgeous out and there are lots of people milling about enjoying the beautiful day. I'm leaning on a wooden fence that's anchored in the sand and I'm deep in thought, staring out at the ocean. I'm pissed off because I lost at black jack. I don't like losing. But this time I made two mistakes and it cost me big time. Shit! I'm disgusted with myself. But after immersing myself for over three decades in the world of psychology and taking pride in my counseling skills, I am now very confident of my ability to put my frustration aside and not let it show at all.

Just then, Charlotte leans over and whispers in my ear, "You know it's not fun being with you when you're like this."

Huh? I'm stunned by her words. My eyes widen as I briefly glance back at her, but then I'm totally blown away when I hear my own words come flying out of my mouth. "You're right. It's not fun for me either."

Whoa! What happened to all my righteous defensiveness? It was inexplicably gone. All those years spent protecting my stubborn ego when it came to my gambling. But now something had obviously changed in me, and I was now copping to having a gambling problem. Problem? Well, let's call it an issue. And the issue was not about how much money I lost, but how my obsession with winning and losing was taking me away from my life. It felt like something deep inside of me was tired of the same old game. Some higher power in me was rebelling against my rebellious nature. Something inside of me wanted more for my life and, somehow, my stubborn defensiveness was exposed to me for the first time as simply boring and shallow. Wow!

Charlotte and I talked for a long time that afternoon about what we wanted for our future and how my obsession about winning and losing had often interfered. I made a commitment to us both, right then and there, that my priorities would never again have gambling at the top of the list. I could feel things beginning to shift, but I knew I was going to need to work at staying more conscious from now on. Not such an easy task. But my life was calling me. I really wanted to have a good time with this amazing woman who loved me. I wanted to reclaim the ability to enjoy the beautiful beach, the Atlantic City boardwalk, the good restaurants, and the night life at the hotels. I told her that I was still going to gamble because I deeply loved something about it, but I would no longer allow my testosterone-filled desperado image of myself to hold me hostage anymore. It wasn't going to be that easy I knew, but I somehow believed that I could actually change my old ways. I didn't have to hold onto the old fantasy, that someday I would break the bank at a casino. I used to think that the only way I could get the imagined tattoo of "loser" off my chest was to go into the casino and walk out with way more money than I came in with. I didn't know how to lose with grace. I only knew to slay the dragon or be devoured by the monster. That, my fellow gamblers, was my twisted picture of what a winner was. Kill or be killed. Go in with guns a-blazing and may the best man win. Images of Davy Crockett with his rifle, Ole Betsy, and his Jim Bowie knife making his last stand until the Santa Ana army overwhelmed him. Or visions of Custer's last stand as the burning arrows from the Indians set the wagon train on fire. That's the stuff I grew up with and it was still in me ... and my bet is that it's in all of you, too. Were they really heroes or were they victims? Were they winners or losers? What do you think?

After that eye-opening and mind-altering experience in Atlantic City, I decided to write this book. My intention is to guide my gambling loving brothers and sisters as well as myself toward a healthy love of gambling. That's right. Healthy. This book will not make you feel guilty because you love to take risks. You won't get any sermons here about how you ruined your life and how you are a horrible sinner because you like to wager some money.

You also won't get tips on how to win either. There are more than enough books about that.

Allow me to guide you to a higher, more conscious road, away from any negativity about gambling and toward a better understanding of the energies and emotions that motivate us to want to take risks.

First of all, let me be clear about one thing: Everybody gambles. Most people, though, don't think of it as gambling. But it is. Am I just playing with semantics? I don't think so. Everybody makes numerous decisions each day of their lives. Some of those choices work out well, while others turn out to be disasters. Some of those decisions are minor, like getting stuck in traffic because you tried another route instead of your regular route. Oh, well. No big deal. However, some decisions turn out to be major, like buying a house, having surgery, or getting involved in a new relationship. If those decisions don't work out, our lives are deeply affected in a negative way. Those decisions or choices are gambles because you hope for the best but you really don't know how it's all going to work out. Right? And sometimes we win—the house is great, the surgery went well and our lives are better off, or the new relationship is delicious. And sometimes we lose—the house has problems we did not foresee, the surgery did not go well and there were unexpected complications, or the new relationship is fraught with conflict and pain.

So now, I give you permission to stand tall and proud when others try to make you feel guilty about your gambling. Be firm and don't bother listening to any of that nonsense. Remember ... everybody gambles, whether one admits it or not!

Now, with that monkey off your back, we can start looking at the energy that drives all of us to take risks every day, especially when we are totally unsure of the outcome. After all my years as a therapist, I realize now that the juice of life takes place in the land of uncertainty. The unknown is deeply connected to the mystery of life. There's excitement and anticipation, as well as some anxiety, when we are not sure of the outcome. Gamblers understand this on some intuitive level, even if they may not be aware of it. But now, we can celebrate our persistent desire to journey into that land of uncertainty. And, personally, I feel sorry for all the people who are just too scared to risk anything. Their lives are ordered, secure, safe and, I believe, incredibly dull, but many of them seem to have no problem acting righteous toward those of us who gamble. We all are blessed with free will and we each get to choose the kind of life we desire. I will continue to wish those people well. However, I think the biggest mistake anyone can make in life is to never take a chance. As the saying goes, "Sometimes you win, sometimes you lose, and sometimes you get rained out." But you've got to show up to play. It's so important to remember that life offers us precious jewels when we stay open to the mystery. Remember the CHANCE card in Monopoly? The big question mark of life has unlimited possibilities if you are willing to take a chance.

I must add a disclaimer here about gambling. Those who have a gambling addiction really do need some help. This is true about anybody enslaved by any addiction, whether gambling, drugs, alcohol, cigarettes, or any of a myriad of other addictions. The problem is not the gambling. The problem is the addictive personality disorder. I wish the best for all people who are struggling with any addiction disorder and hope they are blessed with strong, loving, supportive people in their lives who help guide them toward freedom from the addiction.

In closing, the following chapters in this book are filled with true stories of my history with gambling from childhood up to the present, along with some ideas and helpful tips to think about regarding those experiences. The amount of money involved in those events is really insignificant, although that always appears to be the main drive for gambling. I sincerely hope you enjoy the stories. More importantly, though, my wish is that you are able to glean some insights into what motivated me and what currently motivates you toward a life of risk taking and gambling. Blessings to you all. May each of you hit the big jackpot you've been seeking right after you finish this book.

CHAPTER 1

MY STOCK MARKET
MAGIC CARPET RIDE

"You gotta know when to hold 'em, know when to fold 'em,
Know when to walk away, know when to run.
You don't count your money when you're sittin' at the table,
There'll be time enough for countin' when the dealing's done."
The Gambler, Kenny Rogers

Gambling has always been exciting for me, whether I was in direct competition in a game of pocket billiards with a worthy opponent or if I was immersed in betting on horses or professional sports. In fact I must say that gambling is never ever boring for me. If I make a small wager on a football game, I immediately perk up and start rooting for the team I bet. Doesn't matter which club it is. It could be the worst team in the world, but if I find a reason to bet on them, I am instantly transformed into a cheering fan of that team. Depending on how much I wagered, I'm either happily engaged in the game or wildly passionate.

Something in me comes alive when I place a bet. Don't know if this is true, but a friend once told me that placing a bet triggers the same physiological reaction in the brain as winning the bet. Maybe that's why I almost always get that adrenalin rush and feel happy when I make a wager. Doesn't matter if the bet turns out to be a win or a loss, it's still a rush. Somebody also told me that sneezing triggers the same body reaction as orgasm and, although I do get a rush whenever I sneeze, I'm not exactly sure about the intensity levels being the same. However, I have a friend who sneezes six or seven times in a row and boy, does she look relaxed and happy when the sneezing fit is over.

So an uncle of mine died in the early nineties and, much to my surprise, he left me a little inheritance—about sixty thousand dollars. That was the biggest windfall in my life, and I didn't even make a bet on it. How about that? It just came to me out of the blue. *Lucky me*, I thought. *Sixty thousand bucks. Wow!* After the euphoria from receiving the gift wore off, I had to decide what to do with the money. My parents did their best to teach me how to save money by putting it in the bank, like what they did with all the money I got from my bar-mitzvah. That lesson backfired big time because after saving that money for ten years, my first wife buzzed through it in a week. So saving that conventional way was definitely out for me. What to do?

I wasn't so irresponsible as to gamble with it because that would have been clearly the wrong thing to do. I was much smarter than that. I remembered that my uncle had made some money in the stock market, so I decided to look into investing the money in some stocks. I knew nothing but called a local broker who encouraged me to purchase IBM and some other stocks that were pretty "safe." I agreed, and next thing I knew I was a proud owner with some shares in a few different companies.

As a shareholder, I started receiving annual reports in the mail. If I remember correctly, my partner and I looked over only one or two annual reports. It was all Greek to me and from that moment on, all the annual reports went directly to the recycling bin. My only interest was in the stock price. How much were my shares worth and how much was I profiting or losing? I found enough useful information about stocks on the computer and a stock phone line that I had been listening to for a while, and, in some way, it all felt very familiar. There were many similarities to the horse game and the racing form information that I knew very well. All I had to do then was to develop a gambler's understanding of how to read between the lines to really learn how the game was played. The only difference was a horse race is over in a couple of minutes and you know if you won or if you lost. Clean and clear. But with stocks, the race is never ending and you can go to sleep winning and wake up losing. Very unnerving. Then, one day, it hit me out of nowhere. I realized that the stock exchange was the biggest gambling institution in the world. I know there are people who take offense to this kind of thinking, and the idea of long-term investments may be called "low risk" rather than gambling. But to this gambler, if it smells like gambling, tastes like gambling, and looks like gambling, well then, I'm going to call it gambling. It appeared to me to be just like the Wild Wild West. Las Vegas dressed up to look like choir boys. It was time for me to wake up and smell the roses.

I was now awake and aware and I began to immerse myself in the stock market. This felt to me like high stakes gambling and I could have lots of fun, and maybe even make a killing every now and then. Winning was on my mind, and the concern about possibly losing all my inherited money took a backseat. I started buying and selling a bunch of stocks. Some did pretty well, some not so good. But I was up a little and holding my own. Not too bad for a novice. Then, at some point, I bought one hundred shares of Ameri-Trade, a quiet little trading company. The stock price was at twenty-three, so I paid twenty-three hundred for the hundred shares. I was more interested in some other stocks that I owned, however, slowly but surely, Ameri-Trade began to increase in price. I can't remember if I ever thought about buying more shares, but within a few months, the company split twice and now I owned four hundred shares ... and the price continued to rise.

Every day I'd be watching the stock quotes, listening to *CNBC*, buying and selling and talking about stocks with anybody who would listen. I was living a double life; one part of me was functioning as a well respected member of the Tallahassee community, while the other part of me was acting like a hungry vampire who had just tasted blood for the first time. It felt like I had an insatiable appetite and wanted to keep guzzling more and more blood.

It was known as the Tech Bubble and I was right there in it, joyfully riding the wave with a number of tech stocks. Prices were going through wild swings on a daily basis, and I was getting my fill of crazy gambling juice. Ameri-Trade was continuing to skyrocket and was now over fifty dollars a share. I had four hundred shares that were now worth more than twenty thousand dollars and I was dancing every day. But how much more could Ameri-Trade go up? Should I sell now or wait a little longer to see how high it could go? If the stock went down from this point, and I knew that share prices could plunge overnight for any of a number of reasons, I would never forgive myself, so I decided to sell covered calls on my Ameri-Trade shares.

The high stakes casino better known as the Stock Exchange has all kinds of ways to "invest." Options are a form of investing if you think the stock will go higher, or lower for that matter. "Calls" are what you buy if you think higher. "Puts" are the bet if you think the stock will go lower. The options game is too complicated for me to give a whole clear explanation, so I'll just tell you about my adventure with Ameri-Trade.

I sold what is known as "covered calls" on Ameri-Trade. Some unknown person paid me through my broker a nice amount of money to have the right to buy my four hundred shares at fifty five dollars if the stock ever went that high. That money went right into my pocket. Good for me. The option had a two-month deadline on it, which meant if the share price was less than fifty-five on the last day of the option, I would keep my shares as well as all the money the person gave me. Not a bad deal. If the shares were at fifty five or higher, though, the shares would automatically go to the guy who bought the options. Still not a bad deal for me. Well, on the last day, right before the options were to expire, Ameri-Trade went up to fifty five and was taken away from me. I initially felt sad because I loved all the action. But how could I complain? I had just received a total of twenty three thousand dollars for my twenty-three hundred dollar investment. My feeling body was off the charts with emotions from sadness and relief to euphoria and high anxiety. I was feeling out of control emotionally, which was not so good for me since I took pride in helping others who had emotional problems. But my mind was very confused. Should I be feeling happy or sad, nervous or relaxed? It was an upsetting time but I was making lots of money, so I continued. Wouldn't you have done the same?

Within six weeks, Ameri-Trade went up to over seventy-five dollars a share, and, to be honest with you, it was so gut-wrenching to me that I stopped watching the price of the stock, and I have no idea how high it actually went. Although my other stocks were doing well, I raged and wept out loud about giving up Ameri-Trade too prematurely and all that extra cash I would have made, and questioned my fortitude for not having the guts to let it ride. I was making money and torturing myself at the same time, a very strange combination. All the years of being a good counselor finally came through, though, when I created a therapeutic process I called "emotional stop loss." It really helped me and it's helped others over the years. It's a way to have you honestly assess how much your involvement in the stock market is screwing up the rest of your life. If you are in the market and handling the emotional swings in a way that's not too out of control, then staying in the market is all right. If you see that the market is driving you and your family crazy, then it's time to either reduce your holdings or sell everything and get out completely. The tricky part is when you are so deeply ensconced in the market it's very hard to be honest with yourself and your situation. If you have a partner, the emotional stop-loss plan encourages you to ask her or him. Your partner knows for sure how your market trip is affecting your life and the lives of your family members. Getting honest feedback from them will neutralize the power of your denial. It's possible you may not like what you hear, but man up and deal with it. I think to have a winning attitude as well as being a good gambler, you really must be capable of honestly assessing your situation. Otherwise, your denial has the power to destroy you as well as your relationships, and that would be quite unfortunate. And, let's face it: Denial is not just a river in Egypt, as I learned so well on that fateful day on the Atlantic City beach.

I saw an old friend the other day at the track. I heard he had a run of bad luck. He lost his house to foreclosure, he was let go at his office, his car was impounded, and his wife left him. So I went up and said, "Hey, man, how are you doing these days?" He looked at me, smiled, and then calmly replied, "Oh, I'm about even."

CHAPTER 2

FREE FALLING

"Dust in the wind. All we are is dust in the wind." Kansas
You don't know what you've got until you lose it.

Wall Street old-timers had an expression that I tried my very best to honor: "The trend is your friend." It meant that if the whole market was going higher, then the probability was that a majority of the stocks that you owned would also go higher. If the trend was negative for stocks, you had to be aware and act accordingly. After recovering from the wild emotional swings from Ameri-Trade, I did my best to make good decisions about which stocks to buy and sell. I was way ahead thanks to my good fortunes with Ameri-Trade and a number of other stocks that I did well on. I was riding the trend, jumping in and out with stocks every couple of weeks, and it was all based on what they were doing that week—not the smartest way to invest. But I was making money, so who cared if it wasn't sound investing? It was gambling, fast and furious, and I knew it. So what if I hardly knew what the companies actually did? Did it matter that I methodically recycled all the annual reports without turning one page to see what was inside? If the stock went up, I was happy and felt very smart. If the stock went down, I shrugged my shoulders and sold it before I lost too much. It was action twenty-four hours a day and I was dancing with the stars in the biggest casino in the world and winning at it.

Then I made the smartest move in my history with the stock market. I was up over a hundred thousand dollars, so I decided to take about half of the profits and do some needed renovations to the house I bought in Tallahassee. I originally sold some stock worth about twenty-five thousand dollars for a down payment on the house. Now, the money went toward a screened-in porch, an outdoor pool, and enclosing a garage and turning it into two beautiful rooms. I don't even remember which stocks I sold. It didn't matter to me at all, although there was a fleeting moment of sadness when I realized that I was cashing in some chips from the casino and would have fewer chips to continue to play with. However, I was feeling rich, generous, and very pleased with my decision to proceed with the renovations. Looking back, I learned that spending some profits on real bricks and mortar investments helped me connect the dots, so to speak. The stock market casino was a wild ride, but the money I was making could actually benefit my life and the lives of my family members. I wasn't completely lost. I still managed to have one foot in the casino called the stock market while my other foot was still somewhat grounded in reality and the rest of my life. Unfortunately, that didn't last.

While in the Air Force, I was trained to be a weatherman. I loved the wild swings in weather and I loved doing my best to give a good forecast. When I was right, I felt smart. When I blew the forecast completely, I'd just shrug my shoulders and point out the impossible task of predicting the weather. I was in a business where I could enjoy the benefits of being right but I could shirk all responsibility when I was wrong. Not a bad deal. I was fascinated with the intensity of big thunderstorms with all the flashes of lightning and crashes of thunder that shook the ground, along with wind gusts and the heavy torrential rains. Those storms turned me on to the awesome power of Mother Nature. I loved it. Hurricanes, though, I thought, were the ultimate in intense storms. I always watched their destructive power on TV but was never actually in one. What action! When I worked at Homestead Air Force Base in South Florida, I used to pray for hurricanes so we'd have some excitement. But no hurricanes. Most of the time, the weather was beautiful, which resulted in extreme boredom. I hated boredom. I loved action. In the thirty months I worked there at the base, the biggest gust of wind we ever recorded was forty-two MPH. No hurricanes ever came close to Homestead while I was working there. However, twenty years later while living peacefully in Woodstock, New York, I watched in amazement on TV as Hurricane Andrew with top winds of one hundred sixty MPH barreled into the

South Florida area and totally destroyed Homestead AFB. Even though it had been over twenty years since I prayed for hurricanes while working on the base, I still felt a few pangs of guilt. I donated some money to the Red Cross in my attempt to help, but some of my guilty feelings still remain today. Don't mess with Mother Nature. You just never know. It's like playing with fire. Sooner or later, you will get burned.

One day, the market just started turning on a dime. No warning, and for no reason that I could see. The tide started going out. The bubble was busting. But I was new at the game and rationalized beautifully, believing that things of course would turn positive again. Probably pretty soon, I surmised. It felt like a great time to buy more. So I did. I sold some losers and bought some stocks that seemed to be good buys. Not so. The market continued to drop and my stock value was steadily decreasing. The trend now was putting downward pressure on the whole market but I couldn't see it. Feeling crazed with a frenzied energy and now clearly thinking with my head up my ass, I decided that it was the perfect time to go out on margin. My well thought out emotional stop loss plan had totally vanished from my brain and I was officially out of control.

I used to think that buying and selling options was about the craziest way to play the market. But now I jumped into the game of margin, which turned out to be just a little more insane. Who knew? Going out on margin is basically borrowing money from the brokerage firm you are dealing with. They will loan you up to half of the value of your total stock holdings. Isn't that nice of them? So since I was still sure the market would turn around and I still had stocks worth about sixty thousand, I decided to borrow about thirty thousand from the firm. It was scary how easy it was. Want to guess what happened? In a forgiving world, I would have invested that thirty thousand wisely in more stocks, made a nice profit, and happily paid the borrowed money back to the firm. That, however, did not happen to me. I learned the hard way about going out on margin.

Remember the trend is your friend? Well, the market kept going down and my stock value kept decreasing. When my stock value went down to forty thousand, the brokerage firm wanted ten thousand dollars back, since they are legally bound to allow you to only loan up to fifty percent of the client's total holdings. So I grudgingly started selling stock, stocks that I was still convinced would go up soon. Talk about stubborn. I just couldn't believe that my stocks would not increase in value.

To digress for a moment to show you the degree of insanity, I bought one stock at about one hundred dollars per share. When it went down to eighty, I bought more, totally convinced that it would bounce back and I'd make even more money. It kept going down. I bought more at fifty-five and even more at thirty-two, stubbornly refusing to see the light. Of course, it's hard to see the light when you have your head up your ass. To make a long story short, I ended up selling all the shares at ten dollars per share and lost thousands. Another expression on Wall Street is to get out of the way of falling pianos. If you don't, it can really hurt. Well, let me tell you from firsthand experience that it really hurts ... a whole lot.

I made one more dumb and inexcusable move before my dance with the market would come to an abrupt end. A week or so later, as my remaining stocks continued to drift downward, the brokerage firm called me again, this time needing another seven thousand dollars to pay back more of the money I borrowed. I had to make a decision either to sell most of my remaining stocks to pay them off or send them a seven thousand dollar check. After thinking about it for a day, I just couldn't sell my remaining stocks, so I sent them a check. Seven thousand dollars. Wouldn't you know that in less than two months, my holdings were basically reduced to rubble? And looking back, sending them that extra seven thousand bucks was good money pissed away in one last attempt to save face.

Losing all my stock value was horrible, but giving them another seven thousand was obviously the worst move I could have made and my last desperate attempt to avoid feeling like a loser. When you put good money up to try to avoid negative feelings, you are almost guaranteed to lose even more. That, my friends, is a good thing to remember. You have to know when to walk away from the table, even if it feels lousy to walk away. It's the healthier thing to do, or, should I say, it's the less toxic thing to do. We need to remember that the casino will still be there tomorrow. So if you find yourself in a hole, the first thing you must remember is to stop digging. As one of my friends always says, "If you want to play, you have to pay." You have to pay one way or another. Either you lose your stubborn defiance or you lose your shirt. We each get to choose.

Well, I love gambling and I'm going to keep playing. I love life and I love immersing myself in the dance of risk-taking, regardless of the outcome. But the lessons I learned from the market helped me understand the big difference between stupidity and humility. That piece of wisdom was the catalyst that propelled me to take a good, hard look at what happened to me as a child and how I became so immersed in the world of gambling.

CHAPTER 3

WELCOME TO THE
WORLD OF MONEY

"Life is for-giving, not for-getting."

I was born in Brooklyn, New York, on a steamy day in late August of 1948. There was a record-setting heat wave in the New York area that week and maybe that explains why I love the hot weather so much. Maybe? Maybe not. Don't know.... But throughout my childhood, I all too often found myself in hot water and again I don't know if there's any connection. But that's the way it was.

I must have been around five or six when I received my first initiation into the world of money. One hot summer night, I was given my first dollar bill. My parents gave it to me because I had earned it by doing my chores for a whole month. They promised me twenty-five cents each week as an allowance, and although I hadn't received my quarter each of the first three weeks, I still had enthusiasm for doing my chores and knew my parents would of course honor our agreement. Looking back, I now realize that giving me an allowance was a conscious effort on their part to teach me about money and the value of working together as a family. That conscious effort caused more problems for me than if they had done nothing at all. But at least they tried. Their intentions were good, but we all know how the road to Hell was paved with good intentions.

So I cautiously took the dollar in my hand, looked closely at it for a while, then quietly folded it and put it in my pocket. I had a big grin on my face and was feeling pretty good. My parents smiled back at me and all was peaceful in the Klein home ... at least for that night.

The next day, I was playing with a few of my friends, Billy, Johnny, and Ben. I was happy and we were having a great time. I had the dollar bill in my pants pocket and spontaneously asked if they would like me to treat them to some pizza and cokes. They were thrilled. So we walked around the block to Lenny's Pizza. I confidently and proudly ordered four slices and four Cokes for all of us and gave Lenny the dollar. He gave me forty cents back (yes, slices were ten cents and small Cokes were a nickel in the mid-fifties) and I felt great as I ate my pizza and sipped my Coke. The guys loved the snack, were delighted with my generosity, and, after eating, we all went back to playing.

When I came home, my sister, my parents, and I all sat down for dinner. My mother smiled and casually asked me if I still had my dollar bill and I innocently shook my head and showed her the forty cents. I enthusiastically explained to them that I took the guys out for pizza and Cokes, and how much fun it was to treat them. There was a sudden and uncomfortable shift in the energy at the table. Everyone was quiet. I got that uh-oh feeling and thought that I somehow did a very bad thing. Then they started yelling at me and told me the dollar was for me to save, not spend. I remember slinking off to my room feeling confused and really bad about myself.

Looking back on those early days, it took a two-headed, fire-breathing dragon called my parents to twist the innocent mind of their darling little son ... and they did a real good job at that. I learned that money was good to have, but it really wasn't mine to do with as I might have pleased. No. It was mine but I had to only do with it exactly what they expected me to do with it. Otherwise, I could get into trouble, have them yell at me, and maybe even get hit or punished. Not good. So I learned to like money but I also was scared of it.

Years later, I developed a bigger picture about my childhood. I realized my parents grew up during tough times and lived through the horrible Depression in the thirties, as well as the devastation from World War Two. They struggled to make ends meet for years and needed to hold on tight to any money they got. As a young child, I was filled with life, innocence, and generosity, but I was totally vulnerable to be influenced by my parents, the gods who ruled my world. I also loved them dearly and trusted them to teach me all they knew about the world. I never questioned their teaching. I just followed dutifully as their loving and grateful son.

My parents always did the very best they could to raise me and my sister in what they truly believed was a healthy way. Unfortunately, they unintentionally injected me with a healthy dose of their wounds and pain from their past, along with a little basic information about money. And this, the giving as well as the receiving, was done innocently by all in the family in the name of love.

CHAPTER 4

THE SEDUCTIVE TASTE OF WINNING

"Winning isn't everything, it's the only thing"
Coach Vince Lombardi, Green Bay Packers

I can't remember when I received my first ball, but I loved playing with balls, all different kind of balls. Didn't matter how big or how little. Tennis balls, Spalding rubber balls, hard balls, soft balls, basketballs, volleyballs. Balls from morning 'til night. I could create games with a ball that would keep me occupied for hours when I was alone. When I was with a friend or a bunch of guys, we'd play all sorts of different ball games—punchball, softball, stickball, basketball, football, handball, Chinese handball, stoop ball—the list goes on and on. I was pretty good; fast, good eye-to-hand coordination, could catch and throw with the best of them. I was smart, too, and sharp with strategy. I excelled at learning all the nuances of every game. I developed an air of confidence, with maybe just a little taste of arrogance, when playing any game with a ball. My favorite was the variations of baseball, whether it be punchball, softball, or stickball. Hit the ball hard and run like the wind around the bases. Make great catches up against the fence. Uncork a perfect throw to get the guy out at home plate. What a rush!

My friends and I used to watch Major League Baseball on TV and listen to games on the radio. After a good game on the tube, we'd be all juiced up and rush outside, choose up a game, and do our best to emulate our favorite players. My favorite player was Willie McCovey, a power hitting first baseman for the San Francisco Giants. Number forty-four. He was a lefty just like me, and I guess he was one of my first sports heroes. I practiced every move he made when he got into the batter's box. I got it down so well that I felt really powerful when I was at bat. Good results followed, too.

After a game, we'd often go to the local candy store and buy a pack of baseball cards. Five cards with a piece of bubble gum. That's what was in each pack. I'd rip the pack open, stick the gum in my mouth, and closely examine each picture of the Major League player on one side, then study his stats on the back side. The cards had a ton of information about the player and many of the guys would memorize it all, and then proudly share all their knowledge with each other. Too bad we never had a course on baseball statistics in school. We all would have aced the course. No doubt about it!

After what seemed like a very short period of time, all the guys had accumulated their very own private stashes of baseball cards with some duplications. Doubles of Mickey Mantle or Willie Mays were good to keep, but often the duplicates were of some obscure player that nobody cared much about in the first place. Those cards were expendable. So we creatively figured out another game to use the lousy cards, and here's where the gambling energy surfaced.

We'd flip cards against each other, competing to win the other guy's cards. Let's say I flip first and my card lands face up on the ground. The next guy flips and he has to match my face up card. If he flipped a face up card, he'd get to keep both cards. If his flip ended up face down, he'd lose his card. Winner keeps both cards. Sounds benign enough. Right? Well, it didn't take us long to start flipping two or three cards at a time. Winner takes all six cards. And then it got crazier and we'd be flipping five, sometimes ten cards at a time and again winner takes all. So if you practiced your flips and you got pretty good, well, you could clean up and easily come home with thirty or forty cards. Ah, yes. The rush of gambling was in the air and it smelled very sweet to this boy. I loved the competition and the thrill of winning, in spite of the possibility of losing all my cards.

I obviously didn't want to lose my cards, so I practiced on my own until I became really good at either having the cards land face up or face down. I got better and better at doing whatever I needed to win against my opponent. There clearly was a level of skill involved and the excitement of the competition was electric ... especially when I'd win a lot. In the beginning, the new cards would be added to my growing collection of Major League Baseball players and that was a fun benefit of the game. But, after a while, I began to care less and less about which cards I'd win. I cared much more about that delicious feeling of winning. At night, I'd glance at the shoebox packed solid with baseball cards, smile proudly, then push the box under my bed, roll over, and fall asleep feeling like a winner.

I was happy at this time but what I didn't realize was that my enthusiasm for life took a slight distorted turn toward being even more enthusiastic about winning. Competition and the desire to win became a new and important goal in my life, and the baseball cards I was competing for became much less significant.

CHAPTER 5

THE PRINCE OF PITCHING PENNIES

"Every time it rains, it rains pennies from heaven."
The Skyliners

One boring afternoon when I was about five years old, I was aimlessly digging in the dirt in my backyard and talking quietly to the bugs, when I came across two pennies. I brushed the dirt off them and examined them closely, put them in my pocket, smiled, and then went on digging. A minute or so later, I found two more pennies. My eyes widened. I glanced briefly at the new find, then quickly put the two new pennies in my pocket and renewed my digging, but this time with a more intense and determined focus. Were there more pennies just a little deeper in the ground? I kept digging for a long time and kept finding more pennies every so often. I felt excited and was convinced that I was on the verge of striking it rich.

I came back in the house after hours of digging and a heist of about sixteen pennies. It felt like I had discovered a secret source of money that nobody knew about except me. I was bubbling over with enthusiasm, but wasn't sure if I should tell anybody. So I didn't. I kept it to myself. Soon after, I began to have exhilarating dreams of finding lots more money when digging. Although no more pennies were found in that backyard area from all my future digging ventures, I continued to have dreams all throughout the rest of my life of finding buried treasure. To this day, I still have those dreams on occasion and I always wake up with a sweet smile on my face.

A few years later, in the summer of 1957, my family moved. We only moved two blocks away, from a two-family house into an apartment house. It was a simple move, but in a flash, my life changed for the better. The Hamilton House cooperative had two six-story apartment buildings right next to each other with a playground in-between the two buildings. There were ten boys in my age range who lived there and overnight, I instantly had lots of friends to play sports with. When it was nice weather we'd be outside, playing hard and working up a sweat. And when it was cold or rainy, we'd shift our energy and hang out in one of our apartments and play board games like Monopoly, risk, Clue and Candy land. My life was filled between school and after school fun. I fit in very nicely for the most part, but I felt increasingly embarrassed about my religion. We were all Jewish, but all the other guys started going to Hebrew school in the afternoons after regular school to prepare for their upcoming bar-mitzvahs. Not me, though. I had no such plans. My father didn't care much about being an observing Jew, and, in fact, we celebrated Christmas every year, something I really loved but tried to hide from the other guys. The guys found out pretty soon and began to make fun of me until I decided to go to Hebrew school, too. I couldn't care less about having a bar-mitzvah but I needed to get them off my back, and going to Flatbush Jewish Center did just that. So, at the tender age of ten, I started my studies at Hebrew school. Boy, did I learn an amazing amount of new information ... and it wasn't just about being Jewish!

I met and made friends with a bunch of Jewish boys from different neighborhoods. They were all at the school for the same reason: to learn what was important about being Jewish so they could get bar-mitzvahed. Some of the boys who got to school early started pitching pennies to a designated wall. The guy who tossed his penny closest to the wall would win all the other pennies. Whoa! More competition. I watched very closely for a while. This smelled very similar to flipping cards. But this wasn't cards. This was real money and it felt very risky. After reluctantly tossing a few of my own pennies with the guys when they goaded me to get involved, I realized I could make money if I got pretty good at it. *Piece of cake*, I thought. So I spent hours practicing pitching pennies to a wall in my bedroom and then to a wall in the playground until I felt more skilled at the game.

My desire to go to Hebrew school began to increase as I started winning pennies before and sometimes after classes. I was totally intoxicated by the chance to win money and I often did. I usually won fifteen to thirty cents two or three times a week and that money gave me the chance to buy a potato knish, a slice of pizza, or a hot dog on my walk back home. I had become the prince of pitching pennies and I loved it. My unsuspecting mother was very pleased to see how enthusiastic I had become about going to Hebrew school and getting bar-mitzvahed. However, I'm pretty sure she wondered why I appeared to have temporarily lost my big appetite at dinnertime.

Flatbush Jewish Center organized a Saturday morning religious service for the kids who were going through their program. We'd have to get dressed up in suits or jacket and tie and then sit there for about two hours until the service was over. It was encouraged, but not required. I'm sure their desire was to get us to participate and to teach the boys about the Jewish religion, but many of the guys had very little attention for that kind of stuff. Even though it was boring to me, too, I wasn't about to stop going and risk any more belittling attacks from my friends. Not many showed up regularly until the school came up with a good incentive.

The people running the center were pretty shrewd and they figured out a way to entice the students to regularly attend the Saturday morning services. They knew we all loved to go to the movies, so they worked out an arrangement with the Beverly Theater, our local movie house. Each time you came to junior congregation, you would receive a little card at the end of services. When you saved five cards, you could exchange them for a free pass to the movies. So, once again, those in charge held out the carrot and we chased it. It was worth it to me. I loved the movies and I remember many films that my friends and I enjoyed at that theater—from horror movies like *Frankenstein*, to a fun afternoon watching twenty-five color cartoons. I learned to endure the two hours of services on Saturday mornings and, as a side note, I guess I learned a few of the Jewish rituals and songs as well.

At this time in my life, I saw that the adult authorities will often try to manipulate me to get me to comply with their agenda, but if I played my cards right and appeared to them like I had bought their agenda, I'd often find a silver lining that would benefit me as well. Not a bad deal. I could live with that.

I also learned that, although a little risky, there was money to be had. All those other kids had money and they didn't seem too upset when I beat them out of their pennies. All I had to do was to use my discipline to develop the skill needed to rake in the cash.

CHAPTER 6

THE WILD SPIRIT OF TEENAGERS

"I'm just a soul whose intentions are good,
Oh Lord, please don't let me be misunderstood."
The Animals

My bar-mitzvah turned out to be a total success. I handled it like a pro and got all sorts of accolades, including lots of money from my relatives. A whole bunch of checks, some savings bonds and some cold cash, and it was all mine! Well ... not quite. My parents promptly took all the money, smiled smugly, and told me they would put it in a savings account for me. They confidently explained that the money would grow, accumulating interest over the years, and it was something I could count on in the future to help with the finances when I got married. Another wonderful lesson from my parents about money, and we already know how that one worked out.

But now, I was a teenager, and the world was beginning to open up to me like never before. I graduated elementary school with honors and was now going to Montauk Junior High School. I was done with Hebrew school and now, after school, I was either playing softball or stickball at my local schoolyard, or going down to the local bowling alley and bowling a couple of games. Bowling was a sport that I really enjoyed, and the more I practiced, the better I got. It didn't take long though for all the guys at the bowling alley to start bowling for money. Stuck and a buck was the typical bet. If you won, the loser had to give you a dollar and also pay for your game. It made bowling a whole lot more exciting and challenging. We all became even more immersed in the world of competition.

At junior high school lunch break, the guys would eat quickly, then play handball until lunch hour was over. Guess what happened? We started playing handball for money. No surprise ... and the games sometimes got very intense. On the weekends, my friends and I would often get together at night for a "friendly" card game. Poker was the choice most of the time and, of course, it was for money, now for nickels and dimes. If you were really good or you got lucky, you could win ten or fifteen dollars. This may have been the first time I noticed a group of guys acting very nice to each other on the one hand, but on the other hand, doing everything they could do to win money from their friends. It was initially quite confusing, but I learned to play the game according to these strange rules. At least in handball and bowling, you were able to go all out to win with no pretense. Everywhere we went there were guys, and the guys were all gambling.

One time, my friends at the Hamilton House and I were challenged to a softball game by a bunch of teenagers from another neighborhood for five dollars a man. Anytime anybody was ever challenged in those days, you'd feel the mounting peer pressure to meet the challenge, whether you felt competent or not. It was almost like a right of passage, because if you didn't meet the challenge, you'd be seen by all the guys as a chicken or a coward. And, in some strange way, it sometimes felt better to meet the challenge, even if it resulted in a loss, rather than to back away from the competition. We talked it over and then decided to take the challenge. However, this particular challenge was the first time I experienced playing for money as a group. All the other gambling I did before was all about me against the other guy. I definitely liked being totally in charge. When I won I felt great and thought I was hot stuff. When I lost, I'd be pissed off, often at myself, and then be more determined than ever to get better. But now, all of a sudden, it wasn't all on my shoulders. Now we were playing as a group and cheering for each other when things went well, and feeling frustrated or disappointed when one of the guys would screw up an important play. This carried much more tension because nobody wanted to make an error and let the team down.

It was fascinating to see how playing for a little money could cause some guys to step up and play better than ever while other guys would be so tense that they would shrink and their ability suffered greatly. The phrase was called "choking," and some guys got a reputation as a choke artist. Guys would ridicule each other by placing their open hand on their throat in a choking posture. Friends would do this with each other, goofing on each other while exposing each other's weak points. With friends like that, who needed enemies?

I don't think I choked much, but I definitely felt more confident in some games and less confident in others. I never got into bowling for much money because I didn't trust myself to be clutch in tough spots. I wouldn't call it choking. I just wasn't that good as a bowler. Choking is when you are really good in something, but when money is on the line, all of a sudden you feel lots of tension and can't do anything right. And when there was a big audience of peers watching, like a big bowling match, some guys just couldn't handle the pressure. In fact, sometimes we made bets, not based on how good somebody actually was, but on how much they were likely to choke with cash on the line.

In 1963, I started high school and got into a fun routine at the end of the week. Saturday mornings, my friends, Jerry and Neal, and I would take the bus to the Diplomat bowling alley near Flatbush Avenue. The place was always packed with bowlers who loved to gamble. We liked to bowl and, initially, we did just that, but the energy at this bowling alley was more focused on gambling. It was very seductive and we got totally caught up in it. Two good bowlers would be bowling against each other for, let's say five or ten dollars a game, but the ten or twenty guys who were watching would be taking side action, side bets on who they think would win the match. It was electric and you didn't even have to bowl. You could just spend the day betting on or against different bowlers. The bowling alley was jumping with energy on those Saturdays. The lanes were packed and there was always a waiting list to bowl.

In November of that year, President Kennedy was assassinated in Dallas, Texas. The president of the United States, shot dead! The whole country was devastated and in shock. It was a Friday and I remember coming home from school, stunned and overcome with sadness. Jerry and Neal came over my house that afternoon and we sat around for an hour or so, quietly mulling over the horrible news. We felt lost and didn't know what to do, so we agreed to go down to the bowling alley in the morning like our normal Saturday routine. We decided to skip bowling. We were too upset, but we felt like going to the Diplomat to commiserate with the regular guys who we thought might show up with the same intention. So, the next day, we went to the bowling alley and walked in quietly, still feeling overwhelmed by the assassination and all the chaos that followed. We looked around and were totally blown away by what we saw. It was unbelievable. The president of the United States had been assassinated the day before and there we were, standing in a packed bowling alley with guys bowling for money as if nothing had happened. I immediately felt disgusted and outraged for a few minutes, then took some deep breaths, stuffed those feelings, and did my best to relate. We hung out for a while, watched some matches, and talked to some of the other guys. But we at least had the decency and discipline to not gamble that day.

Gambling changed the energy in whatever game was being played. Some guys excelled, others couldn't handle the pressure. Isn't that true about life in general? When the shit hits the fan, some can gut it out as they say, while others just don't have the stomach for it. It's good to honestly assess your fortitude. If you are honest with yourself, you will lose less and win more. The trick is to not get caught up in peer pressure because that can really compromise your clear thinking. In addition, it's good to be immersed in something you love, but it's very important to have the integrity and the discipline to honor your principles, your values, and your boundaries.

"If I am not for myself, then who will be?
If I am only for myself, then what am I?
If not now ... when?"
Rabbi Hillel

CHAPTER 7

EVERY MAN FOR HIMSELF!

All for one and one for all? Not a chance!

The difference between illness and wellness is "I" and "we."

One day, three of my friends and I were walking down McDonald Avenue on a balmy summer afternoon, when we all spotted a ten-dollar bill, just lying right there in the street. Somebody yelled, and the next thing I knew, we were all scrambling around on the ground, fighting each other on the cement for the bill. It was pure chaos and it came out of nowhere. We were four twelve-year-old boys at that time who were good friends and lived in the same building complex, and now we were poking ribs, twisting hands and arms, and pulling each other's hair in a frenzied attempt to be the one who came out of the pile with the bill. I can't recall who got the bill, but I clearly remember that it wasn't me. I didn't get the bill, but I did get a few scrapes and some minor bruises. Whoever it was who came up with the bill quickly put it in his pocket, brushed himself off, and immediately attempted to shift the attention of the guys away from the money he just pocketed. One guy was happy and three guys were pissed off, but we proceeded down the street to our next activity as if it were all part of life in the big city. Crazy, huh?

Looking back, I was fascinated that none of the guys ever brought up the possibility of splitting the money. It was every man for himself when it came to money, and there was no way to have a reasonable conversation about it. If we were thinking as a group of trusted friends instead of four separate desperate individuals coming from deep deprivation, we would have split the money and each would have enjoyed a little jackpot that day. But it wasn't meant to be. This kind of behavior obviously betrayed any trust we had built in each other. And the message was clear: We were solid friends—that is, unless there was a good reason to sell out the guys. In that case, let the best man win. This was what I was growing up with, and it definitely had an influence on me and my values around money and friendship, whether it had to do with bowling, a poker game, or a lone ten-dollar bill lying in the street.

On the other hand, there was the time just a couple of weeks later when my Mom and I went to the local supermarket to pick up some items for dinner. The store was busy and the cashier rang up all our items, took my mother's money, and hurriedly handed her back some change. My Mom stopped, looked at the change in her hand, then to the cash register, and back to her hand with the change. She then pulled out one penny and handed it back to the cashier and said proudly, "You gave me one penny too much." I remembered my feelings of disbelief about my Mom's impeccable integrity while flashing on the guys pitching pennies at Hebrew school and my friends fighting for the ten bucks. Needless to say, I felt completely confused about values regarding money. I knew my mother's values were the more honorable ones to have, but my time was spent more and more with my friends and less with my mother. Peer pressure ruled and integrity, sad to say, took a backseat.

CHAPTER 8

RISKY BUSINESS

Don't complain, organize. Don't get angry, get strong. Don't be scared, be determined.

When I turned fifteen, my older friends began to frequent Ace Billiards, a local poolroom directly above the Beverly Theater on Church Avenue. I wanted to join them, so I started sneaking into the poolroom. You had to be at least sixteen to be allowed in. Sneaking in to places became a trend in my life, since most of my friends were a little older, and even though I was one of the best athletes among our group, I often found myself too young to be legal. The guys running the place knew I wasn't sixteen, but they didn't seem to care that much. I was a paying customer, and they were trying to make their business succeed. However, on occasion, just to make it look good for the cops, they would harass me for a birth certificate to prove that I was of legal age. I hated being hassled. I'd come up with a few weak excuses, like trying to get them to believe that I left my birth certificate at home. I constantly found myself trying to talk them into allowing me to play. I couldn't stand the continual harassment and humiliation, so I eventually bought a fake identification which put an end to their harassing me and my need to sneak around. Even though I was still fifteen and under age, I was then free to focus on learning and enjoying the game of pool.

Pocket billiards intrigued me. Once again, it was a game with balls and I was always great at games with balls. So, in less than a year, I was playing better than most of my older friends and winning money at the game. Chicago or Rotation was the most popular game at that time. You had to try to first make the one ball, and then the two ball and so on until all fifteen balls were pocketed. Six balls were called money balls because if you made those balls, the others in the game would have to pay you some money. Another money game with a little bit of luck, but a game where skill usually prevailed and just another way to gamble and make money. Intrigue quickly turned to competence, and then to a passion for the game as I began to develop into a pretty good player. But now, the stakes were getting bigger in many ways as we were getting older. The guys I played against started playing for a quarter a money ball. If you made four out of the six money balls, you'd get a dollar from the other players. You could make a bunch of money on any given day depending on how the balls bounced.

Besides learning the game of pool, I had to learn how to dodge the junkies who would hang out in the corners of the poolroom and shoot up in the bathroom. This took some skill and cunning, because you had to act nice to them or they would target you with their crazed hostility. However, if you were a little too nice, they'd put their arm around you as if you were a buddy and then they'd start hitting you up for a dime or a quarter whenever they saw you come into the poolroom. It was tricky to navigate the junkies, but I had such a burning desire to keep playing the game of pool, and that alone was strong enough to keep me coming back.

I was like a sponge, absorbing so much new information about the world, but sometimes I had to learn my lessons the hard way. I found out that playing for money with my last two dollars was the kiss of death. I learned through experience that if I only had two bucks in my pocket I couldn't relax, knowing that if I lost one game I'd be broke and couldn't gamble anymore. I lost one too many times under those stress filled conditions until I finally got the message. It had nothing at all to do with my skill level. It had everything to do with the pressure I felt when I had very little money in my pocket to gamble with. So I did my best to have an "emergency" ten dollar bill in my pocket just in case a good game would unfold. Like clockwork I saw that if I gambled with only a few dollars I would play tight and often lose, but if I had an ample amount of cash in my pocket I would be more relaxed and almost always win. Unfortunately though, as a fifteen year old I all too often found myself without extra money. So I reluctantly grew to honor that rule to not play unless I had the money. Sometimes it took real discipline though but it made a big difference in the long run to me. That rule of not playing with my last few dollars stayed with me for years and it's still valid today whenever I gamble.

Ace Billiards was a seedy place, though, and although the game itself was elegant, it always felt a little risky to walk in. The characters who all too often frequented the poolroom ranged from decent guys to hoodlums and junkies. The guys were getting stronger and the fights that would break out every now and then were getting more and more intense. You never knew what you were going to come face to face with on any given day. It could be peaceful one day and the next day you might have to hide under a pool table when some crazies would start throwing pool balls at each other. The balls were rock hard and it would be really terrifying when you'd hear them smashing into the walls. I was growing up and I wanted to do more things out in the world, but on occasion, it could get pretty scary. Sometimes it felt taboo, but incredibly exciting, even though on occasion you had to move fast and get the hell out of there to protect your ass. Ace poolroom, the place where I first learned the game of pocket billiards.

CHAPTER 9

FLORIDA MARTY

Freedom is not the absence of commitment, but the ability to flexibly choose and commit to what a person thinks is best for one's life.

In June of 1965, I graduated high school and in September, went down to South Florida to begin college at the University of Miami. A quick two and a half-hour plane ride from LaGuardia airport to Miami International and I was finally out of Brooklyn and a far distance from my parents, whom I loved dearly but couldn't wait to get away from. I had just turned seventeen and now I was out in the big world and on my own. It felt great. Although I had sincere intentions to study and get a degree, let's just say it didn't quite work out that way.

Miami was a much cleaner city than New York and the weather was tropical. I liked it. I liked it a lot. The beautiful weather, the incredible beaches, the gorgeous girls who were everywhere, the freedom to do whatever my heart desired, but most of all I loved the opportunity to gamble as much as I wanted to. Gambling was everywhere. My eyes widened when I first set foot in the U of M student union. I was blown away to find eight ping pong tables, twelve bowling alleys, and fifteen beautiful pool tables. Unfortunately though, I hardly noticed anything else on the campus. The student union was buzzing with activity, and I was about to meet a whole new group of gamblers, many of whom were soon to become my good buddies.

Just a couple of weeks after I arrived at the university, I met Dom, an older guy from Patterson, New Jersey. One day, he turned me on to horse racing, the sport of kings, and I'll never forget it because the risk I took cost me dearly. He noticed that I had just cashed a fifty dollar check from my parents, my spending cash for the month. He encouraged me to drive down with him to Tropical race track, only a few miles down the road from the university, where he confidently claimed, "There are three great horses running that can't lose." I was into it, and why not. It was just another opportunity to gamble, and I was getting used to winning most of the time.

To make a long story short, Dom convinced me to bet on all three horses, and after all three heavy favorites lost their races, I was broke. My fifty dollars just pissed away on horses that I knew nothing about. I felt like a dummy, a feeling that was totally appropriate for the mess I found myself in, but totally unacceptable to me. I was smart and I knew I had the ability to use my intelligence to my advantage. But instead, I allowed myself to get sucked into something I knew nothing about. I went from being dazed and confused to being furious with myself. It was a very rude welcome to the world of horse racing and pari-mutuel gambling.

I was broke and pissed off, but after licking my wounds for a few days, I decided to teach myself how to read the *Daily Racing Form*, the horse racing newspaper, which had tons of information about the horses who were running each day. The paper had a little tutorial and I learned quickly. My brain took to the information as if it were a cryptic puzzle I was trying to decode. I got to play Sherlock Holmes and find out who done it, or actually who was going to do it! So, one night, I was studying the *Racing Form* for the next day's races, and I found a horse that I liked based on what I had learned. Wiggin's Fork should have been one of the favorites based on my new knowledge, but he was going off at about ten to one. A friend of mine was going to the races the next day so I gave him two dollars to bet on Wiggin's Fork for me. That evening, Gary handed me twenty-four dollars. Wiggin's Fork won his race and I felt pleasantly surprised and a little more confident that I now could hold my own, using my intelligence to pick winners at the race track. I would never again feel like a dummy with regards to horses, or at least that's what I thought.

It took me some time to recover from that horse racing debacle with Dom, but I eventually climbed out of that financial hole by consistently winning in pocket billiards. I was pretty good at pool at that time, but there were many older students who were much better than I was. So I had to pick and choose my games carefully when I played for money, but I still sought out the better players for friendly games because I had a burning desire to get better and better at the game.

Randy, another Jersey guy who was equally good at pool, and I became good friends. We practiced together a lot and we enjoyed the recognition of being seen as two of the better players at the game. Students would often gather quietly and watch us when we played.

One day, we decided to hire Murray, a much older man who knew the game, to teach us the finer aspects of pocket billiards. He taught us straight pool, the game which required the most skill, often played to fifty or seventy-five points. Murray's lessons helped me understand some of the subtleties of the game more. I was so intrigued and genuinely excited about becoming more knowledgeable about this game that I was so passionate about. A couple of weeks later, I decided to go out on my own and bought a few books on pool, which increased my understanding of the game even more. It was a game that required talent and skill to be any good, but intelligence plus discipline to excel. I was methodically getting better and better and gaining in confidence with each learning spurt. Boy, did I love it!

That Christmas, I flew home to Brooklyn and cleaned up when I visited all the poolrooms. The guys couldn't believe how much I improved, and one of them coined the name

"Florida Marty" for me, since I obviously blossomed in Florida. I was feeling great, slowly and confidently walking into many different poolrooms carrying my two-piece pool cue. I was now a recognized player, a somebody in the world of pocket billiards, and I loved every minute of it.

CHAPTER 10

WORTH THE RISK

"... and may the horse be with you."

Yes, it's true. I was officially in college and I actually attended a few classes here and there, especially when there was no important gambling action to be had. In my slightly twisted adolescent mind, the gambling scene was much more exciting than any classes I would ever attend, and that scene became more of a priority to me pretty quickly.

The regular action that took place daily in the student union had some of the guys bowling for money with lots of side bets going on, all kinds of betting opportunities in the poolroom, card games next door at the snack bar or upstairs in the quieter section, and even a couple of guys taking action on the upcoming weekend college and pro football games. This wild atmosphere wasn't happening all the time, but it was the normal action that took place during the week. First stop each morning was to enter the student union. I'd make a B line for the poolroom to check in with my friends. I'd find out about the day's gambling schedule. It was a gambling smorgasbord and I got to choose wisely. I stayed away from the card games, which were mostly hearts and gin rummy, Hollywood style. I was a good poker player and enjoyed those games, but I felt too shaky against good players in gin and never got into hearts. The bowling and football action was fun as a change of pace, but my focus was mostly on the game of pocket billiards. That is, except when it came to horses.

After that hard lesson with my "friend" Dom at Tropical race track and then my subsequent redemption with Wiggin's Fork, I started buying the *Daily Racing Form* on a regular basis, and then I'd carefully go over the past performance charts. If I was going to play the ponies, I was determined to make some intelligent bets. In the early going, I won some, I lost some, but I basically held my own and occasionally walked away with some extra cash. Within a short period of time, I became a convert, seduced by the horse racing game, lured by the possibility of winning lots of money.

I never dreamed of college as an exciting place, but life in Miami was just that. You never knew what betting opportunity would appear from day to day. Some of the poolroom guys would spontaneously cut school on any given afternoon and zoom down to Tropical race track for the last four races on the card. We'd cut our classes in a flash if any of the guys got a tip on a horse. It almost always turned out to be a much more thrilling afternoon activity than listening to a boring lecture in a room with three hundred students. Class energy felt dead. Gambling energy felt juicy and alive. It was my nature to always choose the juicy stuff. Win or lose, it was so much fun.

About ten of the guys were hanging out together at the track one day when Richie, my slightly obnoxious friend, asked me who I liked in the next race. "I like a horse named Niso," I said, still quietly checking out the racing form. I thought Niso had a decent chance to win, and he was going off at twenty-five to one, your typical long shot. Niso was a jet black horse who, based on his past performances, always started off slowly but then put in a strong late kick toward the end of the race. I didn't have a clue if he could actually win, but I thought he was definitely worth the risk of a small wager at that price. Richie knew nothing about the horses but always did his pretentious best to look like a guy who was in the know. "Let's go partners!" Richie barked out loudly to me. I agreed, and we each put one dollar up and bought a two dollar ticket on Niso.

It was a long race and as usual, Niso started off very slowly. At the half mile pole, he was dead last about ten or so lengths off the lead. Richie started jumping up and down, squawking at me and telling everyone that I picked a stiff and that he wanted his money back. All the guys quietly watched his childish antics when I pulled out another dollar from my pocket and threw it at him. He grabbed it off the ground, smiled smugly, and put the dollar bill in his pocket, thinking he pulled a fast one on his friend. Almost immediately after Richie picked up the bill, Niso started his typical late run, methodically passing each horse, and sure enough, he just got up in time to win the race, paying $51.40 on the two dollar bet. Richie looked like an idiot and all the guys were doubled up with laughter while appearing quite impressed with my handicapping. I took my winning ticket, slowly strolled up to the cashier, and collected my winning payoff, put the money in my pocket, and smiled.

My experiences were proving to me that the best combination of all in any gambling situation was intelligence, talent, and a little bit of luck. I also was learning to do my best to avoid idiots who want to be my friend, but if the occasion appears where they manage to humiliate themselves in front of everybody, well, to just sit back and enjoy the moment fully.

CHAPTER 11

TROPICAL TRACK TRAINING

"Today I consider myself the luckiest man on the face of the Earth." Lou Gehrig

One thing led to another, and next thing I knew, I had fallen in love with Tropical race track and gambling on the horses. Sometimes I'd just break into a smile, while sitting quietly on a bench, soaking up the warm rays of the tropical sun and listening to the call of a race. The feeling was deeply soothing, almost from another life, or something I intuitively understood that my father might have enjoyed. I never got to go to the track with my father but I knew he occasionally went with a couple of his friends. I always felt envious of my friends who had dads who took them to the races. I'm pretty sure my mother refused to allow my father to take me out to the race track. I think he felt guilty about his love of gambling and couldn't bring himself to invite me. The sad truth, though, is he didn't even know how to relate to me in any way other than being the intimidating father. Too bad for him and too bad for me. It's possible we could have been good friends, and how that would have changed both of our lives. But it wasn't meant to be.

Eating a bowl of clam chowder and a roll with butter was another one of those very familiar warm feelings I had at Tropical race track. But it wasn't all good fuzzies. There were some frustrating times, some fascinating times, and some sad times, too.

Tropical was the kind of track that got very muddy after a heavy rain, and there were often torrential downpours in Miami. I had a flair for picking winners on muddy tracks, a talent that often paid off nicely. But, one day, I had a painful wake-up call that stunned me. The track was muddy and there were two horses I liked in the upcoming race. So I bet two bucks on Sheet Anchor to win and the other horse to come in second. They finished in exactly that order, and Sheet Anchor paid about thirty-eight dollars for the win, and the other horse paid twenty-one for place. I was happy as a lark as I went to the window and collected fifty-nine bucks. While pocketing my winnings, though, I just happen to glance at the tote board and saw that those who played the two horses together in what I learned was called the perfecta collected a whopping fifteen hundred dollars. What! Holy shit! Fifteen hundred dollars? I had no idea of such a bet, but from that day on, I started playing the perfecta, as well as the straight win bets. As life would have it, in all my years of gambling on the horses, I have never won a perfecta that paid anything close to that kind of money. Oh, well. Live and learn.

A week or so later, my roommate, Gary, asked me if I wanted to go to the track. I decided not to go for some unknown reason, but I knew Fleet Admiral was running in a race and I liked him a lot. So I told Gary about the horse. He didn't seem too interested and in a while took off for the track. As Gary's story goes, when he got to that race, he liked what he thought was the number one horse, Kentucky Jug. He was reading the *Racing Form* and didn't understand why the horse was going off at sixty to one. So he bet five bucks and happily watched the number one horse cross the finish line in front. The horse paid one hundred-twenty dollars on a two dollar bet and a delighted Gary came home with three hundred bucks. Later, Gary looked at the program for that day and noticed that Kentucky Jug was scratched from the race and never ran. Unbelievable! The number one horse that won the race was a horse named, yeah, that's right, Fleet Admiral. I went a little crazy when Gary told me the story, but he took me out to a nice dinner to help ease my pain. The lobster was delicious but I still shake my head when I think of that memory. Sometimes it pays to be oblivious.

Tropical race track closed in 1972. I was back in Miami at that time and decided to go to the last day of racing at the track, in honor of all the memories and the thrilling racing adventures I enjoyed. I felt nostalgic and stayed so I could watch the last race ever run at Tropical. There were twelve horses in the race and I liked number twelve, a horse named Cosmic Bull. The race went off and to my fascination, all the horses broke out of the starting gate except one. Of course, it was Cosmic Bull. There was nothing wrong with the gate. The horse just didn't want to run that day. An omen? Who knows? I wanted to yell and scream to get my money back like my dear friend, Richie, did years back, but instead, I just watched the end of the race, shook my head in disbelief, and tossed my losing ticket on the ground as they closed the race track for good. The next day in the papers, the line for Cosmic Bull read, "Refused." The last horse I bet in the last race ever run at Tropical race track who ran from the last post, post twelve, not only came in dead last but just refused to run. Amazing!

Thanks, Tropical, for educating me on the horses and providing me with some wild adventures. I learned a lot from the days spent on your grounds. And now, Tropical Park is a very nice housing complex with a lovely park. And oh bla dee, oh bla dah, life goes on, la la la la life goes on....

CHAPTER 12

WOULDA COULDA SHOULDA

"I may need to lie down and weep for a while but I'll soon rise to dance another dance." James Michener

Miami had two other well known race tracks back then—Hialeah and Gulfstream. Each track had its own unique identity. Hialeah, used in scenes in a number of Hollywood films, was an elegant, old track with the world famous flight of the flamingoes as a wonderful attraction. In the middle of the race track was a body of water where about fifty or so flamingoes lived. Right around the seventh race, each and every day, flamingoes would take to the sky and fly around the whole track once or twice before settling back down by the water in the center of the track. The flock of pink majestic birds was an incredible sight to see, and, for those moments, everybody at the track stopped to enjoy the spectacular flight of the flamingoes.

On the grounds opposite the track, Hialeah also housed a number of large bird cages with gorgeous parrots and macaws. Some of the birds, while peacefully nibbling on their birdseed, would blurt out words every now and then to the astonishment of those present. Watching and listening to those majestic birds were delightful moments for me. Right next to the bird cages was what appeared to be an old shipwreck, but when you'd walk over the little bridge and into the boat, you would be pleasantly surprised to see a beautiful aquarium with all sorts of tropical fish. Whenever I lost two or three races in a row, I'd circle back to the bird cages and aquarium and enjoy the beauty of Mother Nature. It was a sweet distraction for me and one that I never got tired of.

On the other hand, Gulfstream race track was very different from Hialeah. Everybody there appeared to be totally focused on the horses and betting. I had a number of wild experiences at Gulfstream that I'll never forget.

The Florida Derby is run every March at Gulfstream and it's known as the most important race in Florida leading up to the Kentucky Derby in May. In 1966, I was in my second semester at school and as good students, we would gather in the university poolroom every day talking horses, and for the two weeks leading up to the big race, the conversation was all about the Florida Derby. Kauai King was the hot favorite, and I liked the horse a lot. My friend, "Greg from the country," who drove a big red Cadillac, kept talking about a horse named Williamston Kid. "The Kid," as we called him, had a big finishing kick but would be going off as a long shot, and anyway nobody knew if Kauai King could be beat by any other horse. "Watch out for the Kid!" Greg would yell out with a cautious warning whenever he saw me at school. It was fun banter and it went on everyday right up to the day of the race. I liked Greg but I really didn't give his horse much chance in the race.

Finally, the Saturday of the Florida Derby came, and the track was packed with gamblers and horse lovers in anticipation of the big race. A bunch of the guys from school were there,and everybody was running around, checking out the looks of the horses at the paddock, then rushing over to the betting windows to place their wagers.

I was feeling excited and anxious at the same time, while impatiently waiting my turn on a long line to get my bet down. My confidence in my choice, Kauai King, was dwindling. He was a big favorite, going off at eight to five, and when I looked up at the odds board, I noticed that Williamston Kid was going off at a whopping sixty to one. Kauai King was number four and the Kid was number ten. As my place in line got closer, I pulled out my last twenty dollar bill and was toying with betting ten on each horse. Ten to win on number four, ten to win on number ten. Number ten, number four. Only two minutes to post time and I was next in line, but when I looked at the odds one last time, I saw that Kauai King was still eight to five but the Kid had gone up to ninety to one. Ninety to one? Forget about it. *The horse can't win at ninety to one*, I thought. So I decided to bet all twenty bucks on Kauai King.

The bell rang, the horses sprinted out of the gate, and the race was on. Everybody was yelling and screaming as the horses came down the stretch. Kauai King was leading, but his lead was fading and he looked tired. Two horses came flying on the outside and passed the beaten favorite. I briefly saw the number ten and frantically started praying to the horse racing Gods to not let Williamston Kid win the race. They crossed the finish line together. It was a photo finish. After a minute of nervously biting my nails, they put up the number eleven. Abe's Hope, number eleven, had come in first and Williamston Kid came in a very close second. I took a major sigh of relief, until I saw the numbers of the two horses flashing on the tote board. *Oh, no*, I thought. But sure enough, there was an inquiry into the race. After five or so excruciating minutes, they disqualified Abe's Hope for interference in the stretch and placed number ten, Williamston Kid, as the official winner of the race.

For a two dollar bet, Williamston Kid paid $183.60 to win, $50 to place, and $23 to show. I stared at the tote board for what felt like an eternity, felt a tear trickle down my face, threw my program on the ground with disgust and sat down, feeling very shaky. Sitting there, I figured that if I had bet The Kid to win with the ten bucks, I would have collected $918, a virtual fortune for me in those days. I thought of all the things I might have bought, including my own car. I thought of what went on in my mind while I was on that line. Why didn't I bet number ten? I could have blurted out number ten, along with number four just as easily when I was handing over my twenty dollar bill to the cashier. I was that close! Why didn't I do it? I felt sick to my stomach. What stopped me from making the bet on both horses? I could have even bet two or four lousy bucks on Williamston Kid, just as a saver. But no. Damn it. That kind of money would have most likely changed my life, but it wasn't meant to be. So very close, but just another situation for me that just wasn't meant to be.

I felt bewildered and totally exhausted from thinking about all the ramifications. None of my friends had the Kid either, and we all slowly trudged out of the track and on our way back to the school, completely stunned and drained from the experience.

CHAPTER 13

THE LAND OF UNCERTAINTY

Insanity is doing the same thing over and over again and expecting different results.

The horrible pain from the 1966 Florida Derby settled deep into the marrow of my bones, but, in spite of that, my desire to win at the horses grew. In fact, even though I was going to the University of Miami with the quickly vanishing hopes of getting a good education and making something of myself, there was another goal that attracted more passion in my life. I had been conditioned to picture the life of a successful gambler as a life of ease and one worth striving for. Somehow, making a good living as a gambler had sex appeal. It was something I could be proud of; that is, if I could ever achieve such status. I'm sure this idea was spawned from my Brooklyn adventures and clearly nurtured in college, but for one reason or another, I really took it to heart. And when I was consistently winning in pocket billiards, at the race track, and in poker, which did happen in wild winning streaks, I actually believed that it was possible for me. Was I delusional? Were all my gambling buddies delusional as well or just unsuspecting accomplices in my fantasy?

One year later, I was back at the track about a week before the 1967 version of the Florida Derby. I innocently found myself in another wild race track scene, equally as insane as last year's Florida Derby. Gulfstream Race Track was packed as usual, and the stakes race of that day went off without a hitch, with everybody yelling for their favorite horse. It was a good race, but nothing to write home about. Debonair Dancer came in second, and all those who bet the horse threw their tickets on the ground as their hopes faded into the night. The winner was announced and all appeared normal. A couple of minutes later, an objection against the winner was raised by the jockey of one of the other horses in the race for possible interference. After another grueling five minutes of waiting and anticipation, the winner was disqualified, and Debonair Dancer was placed first. At that point, I saw something I never experienced before at a race track. Hundreds of people were crawling around on the ground searching for discarded tickets with Debonair Dancer's number on them. I joined in the crowd of frenzied searchers and found five tickets worth over fifty dollars. Awesome! Free money. Finder's keepers. It was crazy. Men, women, and children were picking up every ticket on the ground. There were hundreds of losing tickets from prior races. But a few of them were winning tickets with

Debonair Dancer's number on them, and when somebody found a live ticket, they would often scream and others would come running. It was a wild circus filled with every race track emotion possible.

Years ago, I came up with the idea of doing a dissertation on a unique race track phenomenon. I've been to many race tracks and watched hundreds of races. I watched thousands of dollars exchange hands during every race. I've seen people in the throes of every emotion from agony to ecstasy. Yet, not once have I ever witnessed a fist fight or an attempt to steal somebody's money. It's amazing! Of course, there are some security guards and police at every track, but not that many to inhibit a determined thief or some out of control disgruntled gambler. Yet, I have never ever witnessed any violence at a race track. I wonder if perhaps it may be because everybody gets to yell and scream for two minutes every half hour during the running of the races. That comes to about twenty minutes of uninhibited releasing regardless of who wins or loses. Sure, everybody wants to win, but maybe on a deeper level they are all having some kind of meaningful release that has healing qualities regardless of victory or defeat. Who knows? Anyway, I'd love to see that dissertation but I'm not going to be the guy who writes it. I'll just continue to be fascinated by the race track phenomenon.

Over the years, I've learned that the race track is a place where people gather to experience the unknown with the hopes of defying the odds. Enter the land of uncertainty at your own risk. It's also a microcosm of life and society. It's all there. All you have to do is to take a few minutes, pull back a little bit from your obsession with the next race, and look around. You never know what you will find, but I assure you that you will continue to see things you've never seen before. It's either a comedy or a tragedy, depending on your point of view. Take a minute out to smell the roses as they say. Hopefully, you'll enjoy the fragrance.

CHAPTER 14

THE QUEST FOR EXCELLENCE

"Failing to prepare is preparing to fail." UCLA Coach John Wooden

While all my fascination with horse racing was going on, I was methodically developing my ability in pocket billiards. This I knew was my bread and butter, my column of strength, and my god-given talent all rolled up into one beautiful game. I slowly built a useful routine that clearly benefitted my growth in all aspects of playing pool. On most days, I would slowly, confidently walk down the steps in the poolroom and place the set of balls on the table. I'd rack the balls up, then take my two-piece pool cue out of its case and screw it on tight. I'd then pull out some talcum powder and slowly rub it on my hands and up and down the thin part of the cue stick shaft to insure a smooth stroke. Finally, I'd grab some chalk and slowly, carefully chalk up the tip of the cue stick. I was now ready to play.

I practiced on my own as much as I played against others, and it was the practice that helped me think more clearly about the strategies of the game in general. The daily practice also helped me focus more specifically on sharpening my strong points, while developing more consistency in those aspects of the game where I was weak. Weak? Of course, there were parts of the game that I needed to work on. I knew I had natural talent for the game. After all, it was a game with fifteen numbered balls and one white cue ball. Lots of balls! But I wouldn't have gotten too far if I hadn't practiced. So, I worked on my weaknesses instead of trying to avoid them. My goal was always to turn my weak areas into strengths, and I often did just that. Practice was key!

Those who know the game of pool understand that positioning the cue ball for the next shot is the most important skill. Most people can learn to make shots, but very few people ever develop a good grasp of the skill of positioning. I loved the challenge, though, and would deliberately create obstacles on the table during practice sessions to see if I could handle them. Every now and then, I'd clear the table of all the balls and then I'd set up just two balls, the cue ball and one numbered ball for a regular shot. Then I'd ask a friend to place a nine by eleven piece of paper anywhere on the table. It was my job to make the shot and use my positioning skills to have the cue ball come to rest right on the paper. I missed the mark way more than when I actually did it, but that specific practice helped me immensely when I would need to position the cue ball accurately in money games. Those money games were consistently filled with intensity and challenges. In spite of the obvious risk, I felt confident and happy to be right in the middle of all the action.

The poolrooms were filled with characters, and we had a tendency to give names to the regular guys. Some of the names were flattering, some not so nice. But it was all part of the rights of passage in the poolroom. Up in Brooklyn, there was Harry the Egg, Lenny the Hat, Tony Shoes, and Tiny, a guy about three hundred pounds. At the university we had Snake, Shirley Temple, Goggles, Tony the Fish, Bret the Pigeon, Toronado Mike, Rat the Stat, etc. And then there was Florida Marty.

We played straight pool, nine ball, six ball, Chicago, eight ball, one pocket, and even three cushion billiards. Didn't matter which game. When there was money on the line, the game took on a whole different energy. I loved it and could hold my own in any of the games, but I became a force to be reckoned with in straight pool. Even though it was fun to win money, I was continually focusing my attention on the subtleties of the game, and becoming even more passionate about developing excellence at the skills needed to be great. Strange as it sounds, this cost me dearly as I got better.

Hustling was a skill where you would win money from an opponent, but leave them convinced that they should have beaten you. I watched a few of my poolroom buddies do this with incredible deft, hustling people over and over again, winning much more money than I was winning. I knew they were much better than the guys they were playing, but the losers kept coming back for more, time and time again, and donating more of their money to my innocent-looking friends. There used to be a slogan in the poolroom. "For every fish who walks in the door, there are two hustlers waiting to reel him in." I tried this tactic a few times, but I wasn't any good at hustling. I'd be so into playing my best and running balls that eventually nobody wanted to play against me unless I spotted them points. So I did that. Giving guys a ten or twenty point spot in a fifty-point game made it much harder for me, but I loved the challenge and still won a majority of my games. However, I remember, all too often, leaving the poolroom after a tough few hours of games with an extra ten or fifteen bucks while my lesser skilled friends would be leaving with fifty or a hundred dollars. It drove me nuts, but hustling just wasn't my thing.

Although playing for money usually added intensity to our games, the lighter side of life would show up every now and then. I have one amusing memory with a guy named Paul. I spotted him forty balls in a fifty-point game and won fifty to thirty eight. He actually scratched twice, losing two points during the game while I was running rack after rack until I reached fifty. He paid me, looked a little shell-shocked, shook his head, and walked quietly away. Oh, the quiet joy of observing others in awe of your talent. It didn't make me any richer, but it was lots of fun.

Although my father and I never developed a relaxed relationship with each other, I still was able to learn some good things from him. He was a Polar Bear and used to go to the beach throughout the year. I'm sure that my love of nature came from seeing how much he enjoyed the beach as well as the country. My love of clean, neat, and organized also came from seeing how he lived every day of his life. But most of all, I learned from him discipline and the ability to methodically practice on my own toward developing excellence at a skill. This became apparent as I developed excellence at pocket billiards as a young adult, but many years later, that discipline still remains and continues to help me at this time in my life. It's a great quality and in some way it's the finest attribute I received from my father; to take the time to methodically develop excellence at whatever is my heart's desire.

CHAPTER 15

THE SPIRIT OF "COOL"

Don't be a dummy and look like a fool,
Get to a school, learn to be cool!

My friend, Barry, holds a sweet spot in my heart. Years ago, I met him in the student union poolroom at school and we got on pretty well. He was a little nerdy, but in spite of that, he was a good guy and a pretty decent pool player. He was a math major and his best game was three cushion billiards. Barry was keen on all the angles involved in that game and made some pretty impressive shots whenever we played. But Barry had issues. He just wasn't cool. One time, I laughed so hard that I rolled off the couch and fell on the floor in the student union when he told me about a date that he went on the night before. The girl appeared to be pretty hot and she liked Barry. But when he brought her back to his apartment, he just made a drink for her and then proceeded to show her his stamp collection. I knew he was proud of his stamps, but, come on, Barry! And that's all you did with her that night? Unbelievable. And then he just drove her home. When he told me this, I broke into such deep laughter that tears were rolling down my face and my belly was gyrating out of control. "You mean," I pleaded in between gasps of air and bursts of laughter, "you didn't even try to kiss her or bring her into your bedroom?" He glanced at me with a sheepish grin on his face and shook his head in embarrassment. Poor Barry. He just wasn't cool.

I grew up with an image of cool that I desired because I wanted to be seen as cool by all my friends, as well as all the older guys who I thought were really cool. Whether it was a cool hairdo or cool clothes, I wanted it, and worked hard to give the appearance of cool. But it went deeper than looks and clothes. Cool was an energy that you carried, a confidence or an air about yourself that let everybody know you had something special going on.

Paul Newman in *The Hustler* and Steve McQueen in *The Cincinnati Kid* had "it." Sean Connery in all the original James Bond movies had "it." All the gamblers I knew felt they needed to be cool under pressure. That was one of the most important qualities for a good gambler. Making tough shots in a game of pocket billiards with all the money on the line was really cool. Bluffing with a pair of fives and getting guys with much better hands to fold was really cool. And best of all, making a good living as a gambler was seen as the ultimate in "really cool" and something to strive for.

A couple of weeks later, I was in the poolroom and immersed in a big game with Shirley Temple, one of the best players around. There were about twenty guys circled around the table watching us go at it. We were playing for five bucks and there was lots of tension between me and him. I didn't like Temple and thought he was an arrogant, pompous asshole, but he was a damn good player. I knew the match would be tough, but I loved the competition. We were playing straight pool to seventy-five points. It was a close game, nip and tuck, with both of our scores in the mid-fifties. Then, all of a sudden, I looked down at the score and it showed Temple ahead of me by a few more points than I thought it should have been. I got that uh-oh feeling. Something was wrong. I was too sharp with numbers to be mistaken. Both players were in charge of their point score and would adjust their total after their turn. I was sure he had cheated by giving himself too many points. I confronted him on the apparent error but he got defensive and refused to admit anything. I was pissed off but decided to finish the game, thinking that I'd beat the sleazy cheat anyway. Well, from that point on, I played lousy and I lost. Shit! I was so furious with myself for letting his tactics throw me off my game. So I proceeded to take a big risk. I decided to march out of the poolroom in a huff and refused to pay him the five bucks I owed him from the game. He got really pissed off with me and called me out. He pointed to the door and baited me to settle the whole thing outside. I went along, feeling a little anxious but not willing to back down. On the outside, I was oozing bravado, but as I walked outside, I was questioning my fortitude and wondering if giving him the lousy five bucks would have been a much smarter move. After all, he was a little bigger than me and I was much better as a lover than as a fighter. All these thoughts were surfacing but I had backed myself into a corner and I couldn't change my mind now. It would have looked very bad to all the guys and I desperately needed to maintain the image of cool that I had worked so hard to develop.

So there we were, Shirley Temple and Florida Marty, staring daggers at each other, with all the guys encircling us in a typical macho scene, looking like a pack of hungry dogs slowly waiting in anticipation to move in for the kill. I was feeling sick to my stomach.

Just before we were about to start swinging at each other, Barry stepped in to the circle and said to Shirley Temple, "Just how do you think you're going to get the money from Marty?" Temple barked, "I'm going to knock him down and take it off his body!" Barry looked intensely at Temple, shook his head slowly, spoke softly, but in no uncertain terms and said, "Oh, no, you're not! If you think I'm gonna stand around and let you take the money off him, you're nuts. If you want the money that bad, you're gonna have to go through me as well."

Shirley Temple glanced at me, then back to Barry, thought for a moment, and then turned and slowly walked away. The confrontation was over. All the so-called "cool" guys and my other friends appeared to be a bit disappointed. They were all looking for some action. On the other hand, I was elated, although I maintained a tough guy face. But inside, I was deeply grateful for Barry, who stepped up big time to support me and to interrupt what could have been a messy scene. Don't know what would have happened if he didn't step in like that, but my guess is it wouldn't have been very pretty.

Barry helped me avoid some body wounds, but most of all, his actions helped me keep my cool image intact. I did my best over the years to sustain that cool image because it meant so much to me. Recently, though, I started questioning things. What really is "cool" about and why do I even care what people think of me? This was a big shift in my thinking process, probably a result of all the hard work I put in over the years toward establishing a healthy image of myself. I'm not sure which came first, being at peace with myself or not caring what people thought about me. But as irony has it, it appears that since I let go of that need to look "cool," now more people than ever before are treating me as if I'm something special. Interesting. Anyway, after that experience at the university, my idea of cool shifted big time. Barry, in spite of his other issues, was now seen by me as my new standard for "cool."

CHAPTER 16

HERE TODAY, GONE TOMORROW!

Change is inevitable. Those who welcome change are usually happier people.

As if horses and pool weren't enough action, a bunch of the guys started going out at night to Miami Jai-Alai, a beautiful athletic sport brought over from the Basque country in Spain. The rules were similar to handball, except there were usually eight teams going off at different odds and you could bet on it. I once again found myself in a gambler's wonderland, this time at night in an elegant indoor auditorium called the Miami Jai-Alai fronton. There was so much to learn, and I was soaking up all the nuances of this new exciting form of gambling. The players would catch the ball, known as a *pelota*, in a wicker-like basket called a *cesta*, which was attached to the player's right arms. The game was played on a smooth cementlike surface about 180 feet long with a wire mesh curtain separating the players and the audience. The Jai-

Alai players were amazing athletes that would make awesome catches and return the *pelota* often at speeds of one hundred miles an hour. The game was fast and furious, and the place was electric with sellouts almost every Friday and Saturday nights. Jai-Alai was much more than a sport to gamble on for many of those who attended. There was an elegance to the place, and people commonly dressed up to go out for a special evening at Miami Jai-alai. In fact, you didn't have to bet. You could just sit back, sip a drink, and enjoy the game and all its beauty.

I was mesmerized by the beautiful game of jai-alai. Once again, though, I had to deal with the age thing. You had to be twenty-one to be allowed in. Although I was underage and officially not allowed in, I usually found a way to slip by the security guards with little difficulty. But the sneaking around dance I had to live out kept me from being totally involved in the game at times, as I found myself all too often on edge, trying to avoid the ominous gaze of the security guards so I wouldn't get thrown out.

In spite of my personal dance with the security guards, there was a period of a couple of fun-filled months when about twenty or so guys from the university would gather every night in the same section and carry on, discussing who they were going to bet, and then goofing on each other during the games all throughout the evening. It was social, it was exciting, and it was gambling and I loved it.

The most popular bet was called a *quiniela*. To win a *quiniela* bet, you had to have the team who came in first coupled in your bet with the team who came in second.

Didn't matter which one came in first or second. You'd win your bet either way. The payoffs were often quite generous, which made the gambling all the more exciting. The game was very different from watching a horse race, which, from start to finish, usually took about two minutes in the longest races. Some jai-alai games could last for fifteen or even twenty minutes, with the crowd frantically yelling on each point. I also loved the pinglike sound of the *pelota* hitting the wall, the grunts of the incredibly athletic players making great shots, and the constant roar of the crowd.

Although jai-alai was fun and exciting, I eventually realized anybody could win any game at any time, which made it very hard to have confidence when making a bet. So the game slowly became more about a fun evening rather than a place you could think about making a big score. It didn't matter to me, though. I always wanted to win, but I so enjoyed an evening at jai-alai no matter what.

We also immersed ourselves in dog racing for a period of time. Jai-alai had a classier aura, but there was no consistency, whereas the dogs had somewhat reliable past performance charts to go over, and their ability to win races followed some logic and reason. But the dog track just didn't hold my interest. It was always fun when I won, but all the races were under one minute and I much preferred the elegance of an evening at the Miami Jai-Alai Fronton or a day at the flats.

However, there were days when we threw caution to the wind and totally immersed ourselves in all three. I remember a few very special gambling marathons with my sidekicks, Hank and Gary. We'd get up, have a little breakfast while going over the racing form for the horses who were running that day. We'd drive over to the track around noon for the ten races, have a little dinner, hop over to Flagler dog track for the twelve dog races, then complete the trifecta by zooming over to Miami for the last three games of jai-alai. Those were wild and crazy days, truly a gambler's paradise. With twenty-five betting opportunities in one day, we would watch our bankrolls go up and down like yoyos with absolutely no idea how we would fare at the end of the day. It was during these stretches that I learned another very important lesson that has helped me relax over the years about winning and losing. I learned that when I won, I would get to eat lobster or prime ribs of beef, and when I lost, I'd eat spaghetti or beans and rice. But I knew that I would always eat.

One memory, though, stands out for me regarding my dog racing adventures. I had a friend, Adrian, who was seriously into betting on the dogs. He was unassuming, smart, and always focused. Nothing seemed to be able to shake him. Although I liked him, I thought he was a little strange. Over a period of a few months, he quietly and methodically accumulated a few thousand dollars in winnings. I was impressed when I found this out, but then I was fascinated when he told me what he intended to do with the winnings. He was from Romania, going to school on a scholarship, and he was methodically putting the winnings in the bank so he could save up enough money to send for his sister and help her leave Romania and come to America. Wow! Maybe having a more meaningful intention than just winning money to soothe our egos actually helps us become winners in some magical way. Who knows? But I do think it's something to wonder about.

I recently have been spending winters in the South Florida area and, on a very sad note, most likely due to the onset of internet gambling and the legalization of casinos in Florida, the incredible, electric atmosphere at Miami Jai-alai from years past is now just a memory. I still enjoy going to jai-alai, but the energy of the place now is very different from the way it used to be. They never play at night with the current program, and the weekend nights used to be the hottest place to go in town. And, if you're lucky, there may be one or two hundred hard core gamblers in the audience, a far cry from the beautiful, old and elegant fronton being packed to the gills with such a diverse and passionate group of people, cheering their favorite players on to victory. But times are constantly changing, and it's our job to do our best to flow with the changes, whether we like them or not. In fact, those who are able to flow with the changes that life inevitably will bring us tend to be happier people. But there's nothing wrong with remembering the good old days with a sweet sense of nostalgia. La Dolce vita! Some of those days were really sweet and they really did happen! And, yes, I remember them well.

CHAPTER 17

THE LUCK OF FLORIDA MARTY

"Here's to those who wish me well and all the rest can go to hell."

After three semesters at the University of Miami, I took a major gamble, dropped out of college, and, in April of 1967, joined the Air Force. I knew it was risky business, but it felt like the best available choice for my next step in life. I had at that time absolutely no interest in school and started feeling guilty about spending my parent's hard earned money just so I could goof off and gamble. I thought it would be smarter to enlist rather than wait to get drafted and then most likely get shipped off to Vietnam. I was repulsed by war in general and had zero interest in participating in the war in Vietnam or, for that matter, any war. Sometimes we make bets and we initially think we won, but once all the cards are played, we sadly discover that it didn't work out exactly the way we thought it would. When we take risks, we really never know how it's all going to unfold. That's the essence of risk taking.

So I went from a late night of gambling at Miami jai-alai to a morning plane ride to San Antonio, Texas, and arrived at Lackland AFB late that next night. Early the next morning, we were marched over to the barber and our heads were shaved. Good-bye personality. I woke up the next morning, stared at myself in the bathroom mirror, not quite sure if I was really looking at myself or if the image in the mirror was a totally different human being. A few deep sighs and then the acknowledgement that, yes, it was still me, but a very strange-looking version.

After six weeks of basic training and getting into great shape, which I actually enjoyed, I was shipped out to Chanute AFB in Southern Illinois, where I spent five months learning meteorology, the study of weather. Learning about weather was a childhood dream. I was elated. I was also thrilled and intrigued because there was a group of guys who liked to gamble. This is where I excelled in poker, winning lots of money from all the guys who thought they knew how to play. Gus and the Beamer, two of my gambling buddies on the base, were also good players, and the three of us thrived as the top guns in our little world. I remember a number of times when, at two in the morning, the three of us were playing against each other, but with other people's money. Sweet surrender. There always seemed to be a trail of guys who came in to the game, lost their money, and disappeared, only to come back another night for another chance to donate to our wallets. I was fascinated to see how many guys liked the challenge of going up against us, even though they would usually walk away with hardly any money. They wanted to try to take a shot at the big boys. It was all right by us. We didn't have any scruples. Cash was king and if they had cash, they would get a seat at the table.

When we couldn't play poker, we created another fun game to keep up the action. Liar's poker was big in our squadron. In this game, each person takes one of their dollar bills and uses the serial numbers to declare a poker hand, like four sevens. The two players go back and forth, needing to either declare a higher hand or to challenge the other. But if you declared four sevens, you didn't need all four sevens in your hand. When challenged, you both must show each other's numbers. If I have only three sevens in my hand but the other guy has one seven, the total of four sevens would make me a winner. Bluffing was a great strategy in this form of gambling, and I often had the guys so confused that they didn't know if they were coming or going.

Once everybody got the hang of liar's poker, guys were pulling out dollar bills whenever there was a spare minute. Our ability to gamble became more flexible. We'd gamble at meals, between classes, in the barracks, and actually on occasion when we were marching to and from places. It was crazy and totally unacceptable behavior for good soldiers, but it added lots of juice to what otherwise would have been a long string of very boring days and nights. There were many times my uniform pants were bulging with crumpled up one dollar bills and my face had a satisfied somewhat smug look. Hey! What's a guy to do? I was good at the game, pretty darn crafty, and I kept winning.

Every week, the base would have pocket billiard tournaments, but after easily winning the first three tournaments I entered, I quickly lost all interest. There was absolutely no competition for me. I would have kept playing if money was the prize, but I received shirts instead. I initially checked out the shirts but they weren't my style, so I gave them away. Those who watched me play pool were obviously impressed with my skills. Some would cautiously come over and ask me for a few tips to help improve their game. I'd show them a thing or two but didn't spend much time with them. Although I didn't hang out with those guys, the respect and admiration for my skills I received from them always felt good.

I completed weather school in good standing and now was a certified weatherman, a childhood dream. After my stint at Chanute AFB, I moved on to Homestead AFB, only twenty miles south of Miami, Florida. Turns out that base needed a weatherman and I just happened to be available. Can you believe that? And, honestly, I didn't get help from any politicians. It just worked out that way. It was pure luck. So I landed just twenty miles south of the U of Miami, my old stomping ground, the place where I had lots of friends, and waiting for me were all the gambling establishments that I already knew so well. I felt pretty cocky, was hot and lucky, and I thought nothing could go wrong.

CHAPTER 18

FROM INVINCIBILITY TO HUMILITY

"When I am simply grateful, life is simply great!"
Dr. Jill Bolte Taylor

Before my assignment at Homestead AFB in South Florida started, I had an eye-opening experience that may have been a sign of what was to come for me. But I was clueless at that time and could not read the writing on the wall. Truth be told, though, I don't know if it would have mattered if I did have a clue.

I had been feeling pretty cocky as a gambler and a pool player when I left Chanute Air Force Base and spent two weeks back in Brooklyn. It had been my first furlough before moving on to Homestead AFB.

So, one night, I went down to Spinelli's poolroom on Flatbush Avenue and started practicing. Two older guys came over to my table, watched for a while, and then one of them asked me to play for money. "Sure. Nine Ball all right?" I queried. The guy nodded and we started playing. It was a Saturday night and the place was packed. The guy was pretty good, but really not too much of a match for me. So I was winning. Fifty bucks. A hundred bucks. We played for a few hours and I was up about two hundred dollars. At that point, I looked around and noticed that we were now the only ones left in the poolroom, except for the old man who ran the place. I turned back and saw my opponent pulling something out of his pocket. He gently placed it on the side of the pool table so I could see it clearly. It was a gun. Holy shit! A gun? The guy focused his gaze intensely at me, briefly glanced down to the gun, and quickly back to me and smiled. He announced that he wanted to play the next game, the last game for double or nothing. One game for two hundred dollars? Did I have a choice? I looked over to the gun again, looked back to the guy, and quietly agreed. I would have played better than ever for two hundred bucks, and there was no way in hell that he could have beaten me. But under those circumstances, I knew what I had to do. I had to lose. So even though it killed me to hold back, I did. The guy made the winning shot, turned to me, came over, and put his arm around me. "Nice game!" he blurted out. "Yeah. Nice game." I replied, subdued and with a nervous belly. I quietly put my cue stick in its case and walked over to pay for the time. The guy told me to forget it. He said since I was such a good sport, he'd cover the cost for playing. I thanked him and left cautiously, hoping that they would not follow me. They didn't. I got home, shook a little, and thought about how cocky I was just a few hours ago and now how grateful I was to just be alive. You just never know.

CHAPTER 19

GAMBLING WITH LIFE

"Hey, I heard your friend won the lottery."
"That's great!"
"Well ... he did win the lottery, but with some of the money, he bought a yacht and the yacht sank."
"Oh, that's terrible."
"Well... he was rescued by the Coast Guard, and while recuperating in the hospital, he fell in love with his nurse."
"Oh, that's great."
"Well... they got married and bought a beautiful house on the beach, but then a hurricane came and washed the house out to sea."
"Oh, that's terrible."
"Well... they wrote a book about the nightmare and it became a best seller."
"Oh, that's great... or is it?"

Homestead AFB was heaven for me. I was working as a weatherman six days and getting three days off. I was hanging out with my school buddies at the university when

I wasn't playing soldier, and, once again, I was happily spending time at the race tracks and Miami jai-alai. I entered a tournament in pocket billiards and won the title of South Florida Amateur Champion for 1968. I beat Mike, a sixteen-year-old pheenom and by far the best young player in the state, in the finals. His talent was over the top, but I used my intelligence combined with my skill to outsmart him and win. I was feeling pretty damn good about myself. Things couldn't get much better ... and in fact, they didn't. Unfortunately for me, they got much worse.

Gambling for money is one thing. But gambling with my life is a whole other ball game. One warm and quiet Florida morning, I strolled down to the weather station and was handed a set of orders for Nha Trang AFB, Vietnam. Shit! Vietnam? I didn't want to go at all. I had thirty days to report, but I just couldn't go. I was stunned beyond belief, actually very scared. But what could I do? Could I find a way out? To make a long story short, I went to a bunch of different doctors and the eye doctor discovered an eye problem and I got a reprieve. I was obviously shaken up by the ordeal but felt very lucky and incredibly relieved when the orders were cancelled. I gambled and won ... at least for the time being.

One thing led to another, though, as usually happens in life, and after three more sets of orders for Vietnam were cancelled, after a medical discharge out of the Air Force, after three eye surgeries and finally after a few more years of slowly losing what vision I had left, I finally went totally blind in 1974. Yeah. Totally blind! I gambled and I lost, big time ... or did I?

CHAPTER 20

THE MYSTERY OF A GOOD TIP

"I must be willing to give up who I am in order to become who I will be."
Albert Einstein

With my loss of vision, my pool playing days were over. My poker playing days were over, too. I now had to resort to gambling on other things and could no longer rely on my skills. This was a hard adjustment and one that still bugs me to this day. But we human beings have an incredible ability to adjust to almost any situation, and I eventually did just that. I moved in to an apartment in the Coconut Grove area of Miami with Ellen, who was to become my first wife. She had a wild side and also enjoyed the crazy, stimulating, dynamic, and sometimes unforgiving world of gambling. We continued our ventures to the race tracks and to jai-alai, which I still was able to enjoy immensely even though I could no longer see the game. Even though I now had no sight, I still had the ability to handicap the horses pretty well, and I could still enjoy the electric energy at jai-alai. And whenever I won and walked away with extra cash, well, it still felt sweet.

Football gambling turned out to be a great diversion for me. Ellen and I moved to Albuquerque, New Mexico, in 1972 and hooked up with a bookie at one of the poolrooms in town. It was a very good year from a gambling point of view, because we almost always bet the Miami Dolphins, and that turned out to be the year they went undefeated. Lucky for us.

We moved back to Miami in 1974 and got involved with a bookie who happened to be a good friend also. I didn't book any football action but I watched week after week as he took bets from about fifty clients. The big game every week was the Monday night game. It was the last chance to make a bet for that weekend, and everybody wanted one last shot. Those who were losing for the weekend were looking to the Monday night game for a chance to bail out and neutralize their losses, while those who were ahead were looking to make a killing and double their winnings. Everybody bet the Monday night game. I noticed one fascinating occurrence that took place on occasion. Usually, the Monday night game was going to be a close match between two good teams, with each team being bet equally, give or take a few hundred bucks. But every now and then, one team looked to be outstanding and almost every bettor would bet that team. Ninety-five percent of the time, though, it was the other team that would either upset the favorite outright or at least cover the point spread on the game. The psychology intrigued me. It was fascinating to me how a point spread on a football game could have such an influence on the public ... but in reverse. Somehow, when everybody felt strongly about betting one team, the other team would consistently prevail. What's that about? Las Vegas makes the football lines and I guess they know what they are doing.

I knew another bookie, too, and I began to compare the point spreads on the games from each bookie. I was intrigued when I discovered that there were often differences. I started to search for big enough discrepancies in the point spreads, which would give me an opportunity to win on both teams. If the final score fell between the two numbers, I'd win both bets. If it didn't, I'd either win one of the bets and push on the other, or only lose the vigorage, ten percent of what I was betting, which would go to the bookie. Not a bad gamble. Every now and then things would work out just beautifully. One time, Oakland was playing Denver, and one bookie had Oakland favored by twelve points. The other bookie had Oakland favored by ten points. I took a shot and bet a hundred bucks on Denver receiving twelve points and I bet Oakland to win with the other bookie only giving ten points. Oakland was ahead twenty-seven to nine late in the game when Denver scored a last minute touchdown to make the score twenty-seven to sixteen. Oakland won by eleven points. How about that! So I won both hundred dollar bets and I was a happy camper. Yes, I could still enjoy the juice of gambling.

Another time, I found a large point spread difference when Texas played Oklahoma in a big college game. The differential was a huge seven points. Oklahoma was favored by twenty points with one bookie, and by twenty-seven points with another. I was decidedly exuberant with that huge point differential, but this time it didn't work out so well. The final score was thirty to nothing, so I lost with one team and won on the other, and just had to cover the vigorage. Too bad. It's really true. You win some and you lose some. But it was clear to me at that time that if I find a way to get the odds in my favor, then I'm bound to win more when I win and lose less when I lose. This sounds simple but it's important. It's exactly what gamblers with winning attitudes do.

Ellen's dad was also into gambling and, one day, he called us with a tip on a horse. I was skeptical at first, feeling a little cautious as we went to the track to bet the horse. What the hell does he know? Well, the horse won easily and paid a pretty good price. *All right!* I thought. A couple of weeks later, he called again with another tip. We dropped everything and went right down to the track and placed a slightly larger wager on the horse. That horse won, too. Wow! I could get used to this. I didn't know where he was getting his tips from, but it was obvious to me that I didn't care. I only cared about winning and leaving the track with more money than what I had when I walked in.

Two weeks later, we got a third call from her dad about a horse named Upper Current. So Ellen, two other friends of ours, and I hurried down to the track. This time, we threw caution to the wind and bet two hundred dollars on the horse, who was going off at twelve to one. The horse came flying on the outside in the stretch, passed all the other horses, and won the race going away. We were delirious, collected over two thousand dollars, and tossed the hundred dollar bills in the car all the way home. That was so much fun. That was also the last tip we ever got from her father. Looking back, I'm still intrigued and bewildered by those tips. What did he know and where did those tips come from anyway? That's something I will never know but will always wonder about.

CHAPTER 21

THE SPIRIT OF BUCKY

The mind is a wonderful servant, but a terrible master

Jack be nimble, Jack be quick, Jack jumped over the candlestick ... and burnt his ass.

A few years later, instead of receiving tips on horses, I found myself in the role of giving tips on horses. I must say I was a pretty good handicapper and I was getting lots of respect from my friends as somebody who could pick the winners with some consistency. Part of me definitely enjoyed the recognition, especially since I was blind, and I constantly got a contact high when friends kept coming to me for some insight on who might win the next race. At one point, I got so cocky with my knowledge of horses that I started writing up a tip sheet once a week and handing it out to my friends. Marty's Little White Sheet! They loved the information and I loved being seen as somebody who was really smart. The euphoria of being seen as a horse racing guru lasted only a little while until life humbled me, as it often does, to those who put themselves on a pedestal.

I was fortunate enough to have a wonderful German shepherd named Bucky, who was incredibly smart and very powerful. I got him when he was five weeks old and only five pounds, but then he grew into a majestic-looking specimen as an adult. He was pure white and about a hundred pounds of solid muscle. We had a great relationship and everybody in town saw how special we were to each other.

So I'm at the track one day with a bunch of friends and there's a horse named Bucky who is running in the next race. I check the *Racing Form* and he's got good numbers. He won his last two races with decent speed ratings and I'm sure he'll be one of the favorites. Some of my friends come running back to me after checking out the horses in the paddock and blurt out that the horse, Bucky, is pure white just like my dog. They are all jumping up and down with excitement and they all run to the windows to bet Bucky. I, on the other hand, am much smarter than my friends about the horse racing game, or at least that's what I think. So I find another horse in the race that looks just as credible as Bucky, but is going off at a nifty six to one. Bucky, as one of the favorites, is going off at a mere two to one and I figure that I can make more money if I bet on the other horse and not on Bucky. So in spite of the logical and overwhelming intuitive calling to bet on Bucky, I decide to bet the other horse. The race goes off and Bucky easily takes the lead and wins the race going away, wire to wire. The horse I bet finishes dead last. All my friends come running over to me after the race, laughing and hugging because they all won money on Bucky. But when they hear that I lost because I bet a different horse, they are initially stunned and appear totally confused. So am I. Totally confused! They get quiet around me and I'm feeling very awkward around them. I am quiet, too, but the noise in my head is very loud and getting louder. The internal recordings are buzzing around my head like bothersome gnats, competing for my attention as they are all screaming. *What are you stupid? You didn't bet a horse named Bucky that had great speed figures? What were you thinking, dummy? I'm an idiot. I'm a loser. What is my problem? There must be something very wrong with me.*

That was a very painful and humbling moment for me. I stopped putting together tip sheets. I quietly took myself off my self-proclaimed pedestal. I had bad dreams about that race for weeks and always woke up sweating and confused about why I didn't bet on Bucky. It wasn't about the money I could have won. No. It was about looking like a fool in the eyes of people who had respected me so much up to that point.

Somewhere down the road, I realized I had the ability to outsmart myself; that I could rationalize and feel strongly about any story that I make up, whether it was connected in any way to reality or not. This kind of thinking is loser mentality. This I surmised could be very costly financially as well as to undermine my confidence and trust in my thinking. So now I at least know that I have the mechanism in place to completely twist reality. My job now is to discern the difference between my clear thinking and this nasty pattern which disguises itself as good thinking. It's obviously just pure rationalizing. I have to keep working at this, and one way I do this is to ask myself if I am trying to outsmart myself. This is winner mentality. KISS means "keep it simple stupid." Gambling can be lots of fun but outsmarting yourself can be very destructive to one's self-confidence. Don't be a wise guy and get caught up in trying to outsmart everybody. There used to be a saying in Brooklyn that "Nice guys end up last." Well, I changed that into "Wise guys can end up last."

CHAPTER 22

THE GAMBLE OF MARRIAGE

"Take My Wife... Please!" Henny Youngman

Fool me once, shame on you. Fool me twice, shame on me.

Since this book is all about gambling and risk taking, I think it makes sense to digress a little and mention one big risk that we all usually make in life—marriage. I am of the belief that most marriages in this country take place as a result of a growing, loving relationship. Both people involved are often filled with love for each other, a joy for their present time life, and an honest enthusiasm for their future life plans. Well, as all of you already know, it all too often does not work out as beautifully as the imagined fantasy. Right? And the results can frequently be much more painful than a loss at the race track.

I've been married three times and subsequently divorced three times. Do I gain points in your book for being an eternal optimist by continuing to chase the beautiful fantasy? Or do I lose points for not learning enough about the shadow side of marriage after the first two times I had to drag my body down that ugly path called divorce? I guess we have to take some responsibility for the paths we have taken, and I am clearly guilty of being a hopeless romantic. May God bless me and all of you who also continue to search for that delicious but elusive fantasy.

The beginnings of those marriages were always filled with bliss and lots of fun; however, the endings were always fraught with pain and confusion. It's a big loss, and it hurts. As if the raw pain isn't enough, we then have to deal with the deep confusion. Confusion strikes at the heart and the mind. What happened? It's like losing a big pot with a full house. How did that happen? How could I have been so unlucky to get such a great hand, only to lose my shirt in the process? Was it my fault? Did I do something wrong? It feels like the perplexed guy who, scratching his head, said, "I cut the rope five times and it's still too short. I just don't understand what I did wrong."

Looking back over my life, though, I must admit that each relationship fed an important part in my growing process at the time and certainly assisted me down the road of my life's path. Ellen, my first wife, was into getting stoned and having lots of fun. I got together with her when I was losing my sight, and stoned days and fun nights were exactly what the doctor ordered, so to speak. Those stoned times with Ellen helped me get through a very difficult period in my life.

Hilary, my second wife, offered me a stable but vibrant, playful, laughter-filled partnership, along with a young son. I didn't know it at the time, but getting a chance to be a caring stepfather has been and still is a very important life-affirming role for me.

Gretchen, my third wife, was a quiet, peace-loving woman who supported my efforts with Southern Springs, a holistic learning center I founded and ran for years in Tallahassee, Florida. It would have been much harder to pull it off without her support. And God bless all three of them because they were all willing to read the racing form to me and indulge me in my love of gambling. Ellen loved the action more than Hilly, and Gretchen loved it the least of all, but they all smiled when I handed over some of my winnings after a good day of gambling. They never once refused the cold cash.

It's a healthier spin to look back and be able to appreciate an ex. Too many people stay angry for years, and that only leads to your own bitterness. If you lost a big hand, you need some time to be pissed off. No problem. Take that time. But then learning to let go is a lot smarter than indulging in punishing yourself with continually recalling the very thing that pissed you off in the first place. It happened. It sucked. But it's over. In fact, it's been over for a long time. Now, the only reason you're feeling pissed off today is because you keep torturing yourself by recalling the past painful memory. Activating old painful memories is called self-abuse. Winners can often allow themselves to feel the sting of a big loss, but then, within a reasonable period of time, they intuitively find a graceful way to let it all go.

In all three marriages, when things soured, it was obviously difficult. The specifics don't really matter, but the bottom line was that I felt ripped off. My guess is they did, too, but I think I did my best to support them on their way out of the relationship and into their future. I however felt like I was dropped like a hot potato once the marriage was done. So what's the lesson here? Probably something like you just never know how people are going to respond when things are hard. You can take it to the bank that when things are going well, everybody is happy and the partnership looks like it was made in heaven. But it's all too often another story when things get tough.

Let's be honest here. Marriage is a gamble because no matter how good it feels in the present time, nobody knows what's going to happen down the road. You gamble that the relationship will grow in healthy ways and you may actually live to experience the feeling of "...happily ever after." But it's like my bookie friend used to say, looking relaxed with a smirk on his face as he took his client's bets, "Nobody knows who's gonna win. Nobody knows."

I don't begrudge my ex-wives anything. They were just doing what they were conditioned to do when going through the end of a relationship—fend for themselves. Survival is the most important thing to all living creatures, including people ... and ex-wives. Well, I also survived and now, I feel much wiser, having had all that life experience. My wisdom has uplifted me to the place of understanding the depth of the phrase, "The coming and the going in all of life." Personally, I'd rather be coming! It's more fun.

CHAPTER 23

THE HEART OF THE HORSEPLAYER

If you keep doing what you did, you'll keep getting what you got.

I've got to hand it to Hilary, though. She was a trooper when it came to supporting my gambling desires. I still flash on crazy times with her when we were into betting on the horses that were racing at Aqueduct or Belmont. There were many days when we drove down to the Kingston OTB (off track betting) to bet on the horses. She would sit cross-legged on the floor reading the racing form to me while Jory, her three-year-old son, would be running around and collecting everybody's losing tickets. All the guys hanging out at OTB paid lots of attention to Jory and I'm sure they all thought her little son was great. I know his presence brought a breath of fresh air to the smoke-filled OTB. But on the other hand, how did I rationalize that it was just fine to be hanging out in a smoke-filled OTB in Kingston with my family? OY! Once again, it's clear that rationalizing can be dangerous to your health ... and to your family's health as well.

As time passed, I developed what I thought was a sensitivity to the energy between Hilary and me, and I believed I could predict winning or losing based on how well we were doing with each other. So if we were getting along, I felt great and had an intuitive feeling that we were going to win that day. If we were not doing so well, I thought it was pretty certain that we would lose. My handicapping was decent in general and I could usually boil a race down to two or three horses. One of them would usually win, and if I was feeling happy, it seemed like I'd almost always pick the right one. If we weren't getting along, I'd somehow almost always pick the horse that lost. Go figure! It was uncanny but, after a while, I just grew to expect those kinds of results.

You might then ask why in the world did I ever gamble when we were not getting along. Good question. The answer is simple. I was stubborn and had a big ego. I wanted to bet on the horses those days and nothing was going to stop me. And I wanted to see if I could pick some winners in an attempt to help break the negative energy between me and Hilary. That was almost as dumb as seeing the past performances of a horse that came in dead last in his last four races but then coming up with a totally ridiculous story about how this time he really had a chance to win. I could do that without blinking an eye. I had an incredible ability to rationalize all kinds of wild scenarios that would give credence to my far-out positive fantasies. To my chagrin, though, I do not have any memories of winning under those conditions. Not one! After all the years that have gone by since then, it's still useful for me to remember that not any one of those wild scenarios that I conjured up ever won for me. In fact, that's why I gave up respecting logic; because I noticed that I could give what appeared to be an ironclad logical explanation that could support either side of an argument. It was all nonsense, though. In time, I learned that logic, or at least my unique form of logic, was flawed. I also learned the quickest way to lose all my money was to rationalize. Once again the negative thought process of rationalizing pops up. Yes, rationalizing can be dangerous to your health ... and to your wallet!

When Hilary and I were getting along, though, winning at the races felt easy. One time, we were spending a weekend in the city with friends and I said, "How about we go to Aqueduct for a few races?" Hilary agreed. We grabbed a cab and next thing you knew, we were walking into the track. What fun. We went over the first two races, bet forty bucks on each race, won both races on two four to one shots, and poof, we were up over three hundred dollars. So I bet forty bucks on the next race and we lost. "Let's go!" I blurted out with a relaxed smile and within the hour, we were back in Manhattan and I had a few hundred extra bucks to play around with. Not bad, huh?

For some reason, it was easy that day to leave the track and not stay for more races to try to make a killing. I was feeling content, a feeling that very few gamblers allow themselves to feel. Anyway, my happy, relaxed attitude lasted even longer than usual because I made the decision to leave the track. Hilary wasn't bugging me to leave. It was solely my decision and I walked away from the seductive lure of more races to bet and the chance of winning even more money. Most gamblers know how hard that can be, but I did it. I call that a very healthy move.

Another time, Barry, my old University of Miami friend who lived in the city, invited me and Hilary to a lunch at the clubhouse at Belmont race track. We agreed and got to have lunch in an exclusive part of the track with Barry's father and mother and two horse trainers. Barry's father owned a few thoroughbreds, so I got to have lunch and talk horses with an interesting group of people. Everyone at the table was impressed when I picked two winners in a row. When I came back to the table after collecting a nice win on the second race, one of the guys asked me if I had a system that helped me pick the winners. They were amazed that this blind guy was doing well and they were losing.

Blindness is very confusing to most people. I have found over the years that people want to either see me as helpless or they want to put me on a pedestal and think that I am a wise man like Merlin the Magician. Sorry. Neither is true. I'm just a regular guy who happens to be blind.

In general, if anybody picks two winners in a row, everybody at the track wants to know what you know that they don't. It's part of the game. I've gone that route, too, always looking to follow a hot hand. The trouble with this logic is the guy who won two in a row may very well have shot his wad and be out of winners for the day, and if you follow his next bet, you could very well be donating more of your money. Too bad, but that does seem to be the way it goes all too often. Use caution when following a gambler who appears to be hot.

Back to the story. So when the guy asked me about how I picked winners, I paused, got quiet, put on a very serious face, and then explained in detail about following the hot trainers, going with the best jockeys, checking out the past performances, the workouts, and the track conditions. The guys were mesmerized with my understanding of the subtleties of the game. Then I took a deep breath and said, "And then, after all that, I simply turn to Hilary and ask her what her favorite color is. Then we see which horse is wearing that color and that's the one we bet on." It wasn't true, but I seized the moment to goof on everybody. I had a stupid expression on my face while Hilary got to watch the others look baffled. The guys were stunned and a little disappointed, but I burst out laughing. Even those in the business are constantly searching for the answer. Problem is there is no answer. When you're hot you're hot, and when you're not you're not, and that's just the way it is.

In fact, every gambler I know is always looking for some edge, some information that gives them an advantage over the other gamblers and a chance for a good winning streak. Some savvy gamblers often referred to as "wise guys" on occasion do cash in big and it's usually because they actually noticed something that helped them go on a winning streak. But like I stated in an earlier chapter, wise guys can often end up last in spite of the occasional hot streak.

There are all sorts of angles you can obsess on, but my favorite used to be searching for a track bias. Every now and then, usually due to weather conditions, a race track will either favor a racing style, speed-favoring tracks or come from behind tracks, or favor the post position the horse will be breaking from. If you know this, you probably will enjoy a temporary edge that can help you win.

One summer at Saratoga race track, I stumbled on a track bias. For some reason I never completely understood, most horses from the outside post positions were doing very well. It didn't matter if they were front runners or horses that came from behind. The horses starting from the outside posts were the places you wanted to put your money. Once I realized this, I started betting the horses with outside posts more heavily. I began to have success and became totally obsessed with the phenomenon. I almost always eliminated all the horses from post one through post six and focused on the four or six outside horses. The logic of past performances was tossed out the window for the most part and I only cared about the ability of the horse after I saw what post he was breaking from. Sometimes, the outside horses would even finish first, second, and third. Big exacta and triple prices were coming in regularly and I was a happy camper. The results were consistent and I was acting like a kid in a candy store.

I'd go home day after day with a bunch more money than I started with and boasted to my friends that they were giving money away at Saratoga. The track bias lasted a couple of weeks that summer, and every day I didn't go to the track during that time I sadly professed was a missed opportunity. That winning streak was so much fun and my confidence for being an excellent handicapper of horses soared. Winning streaks are the best.

On the other hand, losing streaks can really be a drag, but unfortunately they are also a part of the game. I had a friend in the early seventies who bet each game of the New York Knicks and Baltimore Bullets basketball championship series. The series went a full seven games and both teams played great. But my friend was so cold that he actually lost all seven bets. He'd switch back and forth from team to team during the series, trying desperately for a win, but instead he managed to lose every bet. Do you know how hard that is to do? Try to pick seven losers in a row sometime and you'll see. But when you're locked into a losing streak, that's all too often how it goes.

I had one of those painful losing streaks at Saratoga one summer. Everything I touched turned to shit. At one point, I felt desperate to cash any kind of ticket. I just wanted to go up to the window and hand the teller my ticket and have him give me some money. It didn't matter how much. I just desperately felt the need to break the ice so to speak. So I found what I thought was a sure thing. A horse named Baltimore Canyon was going off at two to five in an allowance race with a small field. Just six other horses. He was such a standout and everybody at the track thought this horse couldn't lose. So I made a small wager on Baltimore Canyon, but I decided to bet him to just place rather than to win. I knew I would only win pennies, but I wanted absolutely nothing to interfere with my need to cash a ticket. I thought I covered myself well and that I was being smart, but my small bet turned out to be the kiss of death for the horse.

Well, the horses broke out and, wouldn't you know it, Baltimore Canyon immediately stumbled right out of the gate. He was about fifteen lengths behind after two furlongs. So he made a bold move on the outside in the stretch but came in third, getting photoed out by a nose for second. This I felt was the ultimate insult and simply pathetic. At that point, I wanted to just find a hole and crawl into it. Losing streaks can humble a guy and mess with his mind almost as much as lost love.

I think the horse racing game may be more geared to men than to women. I've known women who like to gamble, but one memory makes me convinced that I might be right about this. It took place on some Father's Day years ago. Hilary agreed to go with our friends, Jerry and his wife, Sharon, to the Albany horse racing tele-theater. It was a nice place to watch the races and bet on them while enjoying a good meal. Jerry and I had been going over the horses for each race, winning a couple and losing a couple, when Hilary asked Jerry, "What motivates you to love gambling on the horses so much?" Just then, before Jerry could respond, the next race went off and

Jerry and I came very close to winning lots of money, but instead we lost everything. It was a photo finish that didn't go in our favor. Jerry and I were doubled over in pain, realizing we just got photoed out of a thousand dollar win. Jerry was moaning out loud when he turned to Hilary and said, "This is what I love about the game." The women looked at each other, shrugged their shoulders, and burst out laughing. To this day, I'm not sure Jerry understood why they were so amused. If you also don't understand, you need to stop reading right now and call a therapist.

CHAPTER 24

PICK-6 GLORY DAYS

"This is the best day ever." Sponge Bob

When Jory, my stepson, was around nine years old, I got into playing the PICK 6 at whichever New York race track was open at the time—Aqueduct, Belmont, or Saratoga. I was definitely seduced. My mind was filled with new and irresistible thoughts. Boatloads of money are coming my way. It really doesn't look that hard. Maybe, just maybe, I can pull it off and win one of these super bets. Maybe tomorrow? Why not?

The PICK 6 is basically a six-horse parlay. For two dollars, you get to pick a horse in six consecutive races. You win the jackpot if all your horses win their races. I was intrigued by this new super bet and learned what I thought was the intelligent way to play the PICK 6. You put up a good amount of money and play multiple horses in some of the races, so if any of your choices win their race, you are still alive for the jackpot. If your ticket has a winner in each of the six races, you then win the big money. Some big gamblers bet hundreds, and even thousands each time they play the PICK-6, but that kind of betting was out of my league. My regular bet was seventy-two bucks. I'd find two races where I liked only one horse that appeared to be a standout, two races where I picked two horses and two races where I had three horses. There were thirty-six combinations with this bet and each cost two dollars; thus, the seventy-two dollar investment.

The PICK 6 is a dream for people who like numbers because there are all kinds of numeric possibilities to bet; however, the bottom line is that you still have to pick the winners in each of the six races. Not so easy. But the wild jackpots of fifty to one hundred thousand dollars or on occasion over a million dollars for a winning PICK 6 ticket happened often enough and still are happening as I write this chapter. The PICK 6 still has a very seductive lure to this day. Thousands of gamblers are continuously attracted to playing it with the dream of cashing in big.

Usually, when I played the PICK-6, I had three or four winners, but three or four winners on a PICK 6 ticket gets you *bupkus*—absolutely nothing. Every now and then, I'd come up with five winners and got back a little cash for the efforts (they pay out a small percentage of the pool for five out of six), but it was never anything to write home about. Nevertheless, I was determined and persisted, hoping for the best.

Hilary and I would drive down to the Kingston OTB in the morning about once a week to make a PICK 6 bet and then we'd go about our business during the day knowing that we could watch the results on TV when we got home in the evening. They would show the recordings of each race and recap the day's results with all payoffs, just in case you were lucky enough to have picked a few winners. Watching the races in our bedroom on our TV was extra fun. I won some and usually lost more, but never won that big pot of gold over the rainbow.

So, one morning when the horses were running at Aqueduct, I bet the PICK 6 and in the late afternoon, I called the OTB phone line to see if any of my horses had won in the earlier races. Good news! One of my horses won each of the first three races in the PICK 6 bet. I got excited and thought I had a realistic chance of actually winning the last three races and hitting the elusive PICK 6. Gamblers—and I am one—are eternal optimists and commonly to a fault. Nowadays, when I start getting that excited optimistic feeling, I usually talk myself down a notch or two since I've been humbled so many times from past experiences. I had one favorite in the fourth race and two horses in each of the last two races of the bet. So, for the next few hours, I was busy and focused on other life activities. Yes, folks, there are other important activities in life besides gambling. Anyway, I knew I'd get to watch the results on the TV in the evening when I got home, so I relaxed and went about my business.

Jory and I were the only two in the house that evening when the racing show came on the TV. We flipped it on and I got him to watch it with me, knowing fully that I already had the first three winners in the bag. I was relaxed, sitting back and smiling as I watched him get excited when one after another of the three winners won their races. Then the fourth race came on and my horse won that race, too. Hmm! Very cool! Jory was jumping all around the room and now I was getting a little juiced myself. The fifth race went off and both my horses finished first and second. Five in a row and only one more race to win my first big PICK 6. This is usually when gamblers become religious and start praying to their God of choice. The prayers usually begin with "Please...." I started biting my nails and went through all my prayers, but quietly to myself. Jory was bouncing around like a Mexican jumping bean, leaping up and down on the bed.... And, let's be honest, I also was feeling that buzz, that amazing adrenalin rush that all my gambling brothers and sisters know oh so well.

The last race was off the charts exciting, especially because, believe it or not, both of my horses ran by the tiring horses in the stretch and came in first and second again. Now, Jory and I were screaming, spinning around and hugging each other on the bed. We were so euphoric, exuberant beyond belief. I finally won the elusive PICK 6 and I got to share the special moment with my stepson. What could be better?

As far as PICK 6 payoffs go, it was pretty small—only thirty-eight hundred dollars. But it was mine. I'll take it. I wasn't complaining. I actually won the damn bet; caught the elusive butterfly.

I remember how sweet that wonderful memory was, as well as driving down the next day with Hilary and Jory to OTB and collecting thirty-eight one hundred dollar bills. It was definitely good juice. It's the reason so many of us love to gamble—to get a shot at cashing in on some big jackpot. But in all honesty, when we received the cash, it felt like no big deal as the money came so easily that day and then disappeared just as easily in the next few weeks. But the amazing moment both Jory and I got to experience with each other has lasted a lifetime and still brings a big smile on my face and a few little tears to my eyes when I recall the memory. It's good for us to remember that those special moments with loved ones are just as valuable, if not more precious, than the fantasy of winning that elusive pot of gold over the rainbow.

CHAPTER 25

Horse Ownership BLUES

"Everything in my life and in the world is perfect just the way it is." Oh bullshit!

In God we trust... and that's about it!

Horse racing is known in the sports world as the sport of kings, and since I always had a deep love of horse racing, I figured I must have been a king in another life. Whether it has to do with either a past life association or that my rising sign is Leo, well, I just don't know, but there always has been a part of my personality that felt very comfortable with being seen as royalty. It really didn't matter much to me that I may have been the only one to see myself in such a light. Somewhere in my adult years, I realized it was that very image of myself which always motivated me toward taking risks, new risks that continually propelled me down the road to my next adventure. At any rate, I decided, for my next gambling adventure, to become a horse owner. I couldn't wait to experience the thrill of watching my horse finish first in a big race, and maybe even collecting a hefty purse for the win. So I did some research and eventually bought into a horse racing syndicate.

Owning thoroughbred horses is a very expensive pastime, and maybe that's why it was known as the sport of kings; because those kings may have been the only ones who could have afforded the expenses. So, a number of years ago, somebody in the business came up with a good idea to get more people involved in owning horses. They started forming horse racing syndicates. With this new angle on the business, a number of people could purchase a percentage of a horse or a group of horses without any one individual being overwhelmed with the exorbitant expenses. Each member of a syndicate would only have to cover a percentage of the expenses for the upkeep on their precious investment while getting to enjoy the thrills of racing thoroughbred horses together as a group.

So I bought a ten percent share of four horses from a horse farm in Columbia County, relatively close to my Ulster County home. Avil Azul (bluebird in Spanish), Company Girl, Chicoli, and Final Scene were the names of the horses. I enthusiastically wrote the first check and became a proud owner of thoroughbreds. I couldn't wait until they would start racing.

Well, as things often go in the horse racing business, I had to wait. Yeah. I had to wait a long time and learn patience until each horse was ready to race. But since I was now a horse owner, I, of course, had to promptly pay the quarterly bills. As it turned out, Avil Azul, the most promising horse, had an injury and needed to be sold on the cheap with the hopes of her becoming a decent brood mare. One down. Three to go. Major bummer! Chicoli and Final Scene finally got to race but they did not do well and were immediately sent into cheap claiming races with no hope of them ever becoming anything much. Two more bite the dust and now there was only one left.

Company Girl, my last shot, appeared to have some potential and she won a couple of races as a two-year old, which was promising. I proudly framed a couple of her pictures and hung them on my living room wall. I started getting excited with anticipation. Maybe she'll be a grade one stakes winner! Who knew? Anything was possible, I told myself. But then something happened that turned me off to the whole business.

Each member owner of the syndicate would be informed when the horses would run so we could go to the track and watch if we had the time. But we were told when the horses would run and we were told what kind of races the horses would be running in; allowance or claiming. We as owners had no say in what would happen to the horse or how the training would take place. That was supposedly all up to the trainer.

I didn't know the trainer from a hole in the wall and I didn't like him making all the important decisions about where to run Company Girl. Too bad for me. When I balked about this, the people who were involved with staying in touch with the owners tried to calm me down, insisting that the trainer knew what was best. Well, maybe he knew what was best for the training of the horse, but I knew a whole bunch about the strategies of racing and the gambling side of the game. It frustrated me to no end that there was no place for me to share my thoughts, which possibly could have been a positive influence. So I just watched and hoped for the best as most silent owners do.

So, one day, I got a call that Company Girl was scheduled to run in a $75,000 claiming race the next day. What? Oh, no! That kind of race was known as a high claiming race for two-year-olds. I hated this news. When horses run in an allowance race, they cannot be bought or sold. Two-year-old allowance races, in my humble opinion, were the only kind of races that Company Girl should have been entered in. When horses run in a claiming race, the horse can be claimed for the claiming price. If the horse is claimed, you no longer own your horse. Somebody else now owns the horse and it's too bad for you. Savvy trainers often place a horse in a claiming race to attempt to "steal" a decent purse without losing their horse. But it's obviously a gamble. Some sharp but tricky trainers also have been known to put a horse into a claiming race with the hopes that some other trainer will think the horse has potential and claim the horse. A clever trainer might do this because his horse may have a health problem that nobody but the trainer knows about, and if the horse gets claimed, the horse will be gone along with the horse's problem. Good luck to the trainer who gets hoodwinked into claiming a "stiff," as they say in the business. Yes, the claiming game is high stakes gambling, and sometimes you win ... and sometimes you lose.

When I heard that Company Girl was going to run in a claiming race, I got that uh-oh feeling and then proceeded to get an upset stomach. I knew the horse had potential and I desperately wanted a chance to stick with her through her racing career ... or at least until her true value was established. At that time, nobody knew what she was worth, and the possibility still existed for her to become something special. I had absolutely no control over what would happen to my horse, so I sat back and hoped for the best. In the breeding business, they often say, "We breed the best with the best and then we hope for the best."

The next day, the race went off and, sure enough, Company girl got claimed by another trainer for the $75,000 claiming price. Gone! My last chance to experience the thrill of owning a winning thoroughbred was gone for good and I was furious. I ranted and raged but to no avail. Those poor people who I yelled at apologized profusely to me, but it didn't matter. Nothing helped. Company Girl was now owned by somebody else and I was once more reduced to being just an observer of the sport of kings.

A few months later, I went to Saratoga and bet some money on Company Girl, who was running that day as the favorite. She won and I collected a few bucks for my efforts. But it was nothing like what I would have felt if I had still owned a part of the horse. I felt bitter about the whole endeavor. Company Girl went on to have what they call in the business a very useful career before she retired. She earned a good chunk of money and I received *gournisht*. Actually that's not true. I received what felt like an ongoing migraine headache from the whole ordeal. I must say, though, that I did learn some things about myself. I learned how much I liked being in control, especially if I had lots of money on the line. I also learned that my trust in others was undermined big time. I remembered that ten dollar bill in the street when all four teenage friends fought with each other for the money. It was every man for himself when it came to money. My trust was initially damaged back then and my trust in others was damaged further by the Company Girl fiasco. I watched my creative mind going through all kinds of scenarios about what went down. One paranoid scenario was that Company Girl's trainer could have been in cahoots with the other trainer who claimed the horse. Maybe that was why he put her in the claiming race in the first place. So she could be taken by the other trainer and somehow they would both benefit from the heist. Highway robbery? Who knew? I'll never know the behind the scenes specifics about what actually took place, but I certainly knew how I felt about the adventure: It made me sick to my stomach. It's one thing when I make a bet and lose. I chose to make that bet and I have to own the bad decision and subsequently handle the feelings that arise from the loss. It's totally another thing when I make a big bet and I lose because of somebody else's screw-up. All throughout this book, I encourage readers to let go of painful gambling experiences. But I'm still growling about this one.

CHAPTER 26

A SPECIAL HEART CONNECTION

"None are so blind as those who will not see,
None are so deaf as those who will not hear,
And none are so numb as those who will not feel."

In 1971, I moved in with Ellen, my first wife, and her three cats. One of the cats was named Motors, a little six-week-old kitten who I immediately fell in love with. He was always purring. We became great buddies over the years and developed a deep and beautiful friendship. I spent the next nineteen years with Motors, more time than I ever spent with any of my wives. We had a special relationship that so often enriched my life and spanned almost two decades, two wives, three geographic locations, and eleven homes. I felt blessed to have such a loving connection with him through all the years, but I also knew that he would not live forever.

On August twenty-fifth of 1990, Motors took his last breath. He died peacefully. Hilary, my wife at the time,

Jory, my stepson, and I gave him a beautiful burial out by our pond in my backyard. It was a day of mourning and I was grieving his death while celebrating his rich life.

The next day, one of my OTB friends came by to see if I wanted to go to Kingston to gamble on the horses. Lenny was a smart but pretty self-centered guy. He had worked for years managing a chicken market in the city and would come up to the country every couple of weeks for a few days to enjoy the change of scenery. I enjoyed going down to OTB with Lenny most of the time. It was fun, engaging, and, occasionally, we'd leave with some decent profits.

But on this particular day, just one day since we buried Motors, I was still filled with grief from losing my special kitty cat and had absolutely no desire to go to bet on horses.

I was floating quietly and peacefully on a raft in the pond and Lenny sat down on the nearby swing. After listening to me describe the little ceremony we had for Motors, Lenny started trying to convince me to go to OTB with him. I initially thought he was doing his best to help me get away for a while, but told him that I just wasn't into it because I was still grieving the loss of my cat. I guess I could have gone down to OTB to bet on a few races, and maybe it would have helped me get my focus away from the sadness I was feeling. But I just couldn't do it. In fact, I didn't want to shift my focus away from my grieving process at all. My sadness was a tribute to Motors, honoring our sweet connection. Apparently, Lenny didn't understand my grieving. He was quiet for a while, but then he began what became a steady barrage of sarcastic comments about how I was way too sensitive about a dead cat. "What are you doing, wasting your time feeling bad?" he barked out while chuckling. "It's just a stupid cat. Nobody cares."

As he persisted with those comments, I slowly shifted from my sad grieving to annoyance, then to frustration and eventually to pure white hot anger. I was furious with Lenny's lack of compassion for me and what appeared to be his self-centered interests. It's possible that after slaughtering hundreds of chickens every day for years at his work that he could have possibly become numb to the preciousness of life. He just didn't get it. I guess that sadly happens to some people, but I wasn't about to change my mind in spite of his efforts.

Lenny continued his attempts at manipulating me until I started screaming at him, totally outraged with his numbed out, detached, and disgustingly inappropriate comments. He finally got the message, slowly got up, and went on his way, not a minute too soon.

I made a decision in that moment while feeling my blood boil that I never wanted anything to do with him again. I only wanted to have friends who had their priorities in a similar place with mine. It's been over twenty years since that afternoon and, although I certainly took a harsh stance that day, I have not missed Lenny much at all. In fact, I think I actually grew up a little that day thanks to Lenny's antics. I became much more focused on what I believe is really important in my life. I'll always love the thrill of gambling, but there are times that the juice I receive from gambling doesn't hold a candle to things that are much more important, like honoring and celebrating the lives of loved ones, family, friends and pets.

CHAPTER 27

LOTTERY LAND

"For those who believe, no words are necessary. For those who do not believe, no amount of words is helpful."
Saint Ignatius of Loyola.

"You gotta believe!" Tug McGraw, New York Mets, 1973

My father always liked to fantasize about someday becoming a millionaire. He grew up very poor in Germany and then lived in the United States during the Depression. He came from poverty and he lived through times of deep deprivation. But he endured, surviving through it all and eventually retired to live his last years in South Florida with comfort and relative financial security. But he never was satisfied. His nagging desire to become a millionaire stayed with him until his death, and that unsatisfied wish caused him all too often to be frustrated, always longing for something he didn't have. I remember when he was in his eighties with failing health. He'd still be talking about winning the lottery. "Dad," I'd say laughing, "if you won the damn lottery tomorrow, you wouldn't change a thing in your life. So why don't you just let go of the fantasy?"

He'd look at me with a funny grin, knowing I was right, but then he'd look down at the floor and shake his head. He couldn't give up the dream.

My father died almost thirty years ago, but I now dutifully continue to carry on his fantasy. I've been intrigued with the state lotteries for years, playing them more than I'd like to admit, but never cashing in on the big jackpot. I'd like to experience that feeling just once in my life, even though that very thought sounds so much like what my father used to say. I've also heard that many lottery winners have not fared so well with their windfalls and many even find a way to piss all the money away and end up broke. Hard to believe. I'm sure I'd be smarter with the money if I won. Just give me a chance to prove it. However, as yet no jackpot for me, but I still dream on as my father did years ago.

In the 1990s, I lived in Tallahassee, Florida, where I organized my own syndicate, but this time it wasn't about horses. I got twenty friends to put up fifty bucks each and form a lottery syndicate. We came up with twenty different sets of numbers and purchased a six-month subscription. The lottery in Florida was drawn twice a week, so we'd win if any of our sets of numbers came in on any of those days during the twenty-six weeks. I watched the results religiously twice a week for the six months but no jackpot. Our group invested one thousand dollars and won back about two hundred dollars in bits and pieces. It was frustrating but we weren't done. I got the same group to ante up again for another six-month subscription, but once again no jackpot. Not even close.

One night, in an attempt to shake up the boring reality of losing, I decided to try a different strategy while watching the lottery drawings. My new plan was to make believe that I had each number as they were drawn so I could get in touch with the euphoric feeling of winning. I was in the house with my wife and two of her children when the drawing came on the TV. They were all busy doing other things and had no interest at all in watching with me. So, after the first number was drawn, I cheered softly. I did the same for the second number. I yelled out "Yes!" a little louder for the third number, doing my best to experience how it might feel in my body sometime down the road when I might actually enjoy the thrill of winning the lottery. I was in touch with the buzz, but when I jumped up after they drew the fourth number, the whole family came rushing into the living room to watch the TV with me. They were all excited as I yelled when the fifth number was drawn, when one of the kids asked me if I was really close to winning. I burst out laughing as they drew the last number. I told them I was just practicing so I could feel how it will be when I win sometime in the future. They got so pissed off at me for getting them excited for no reason and started yelling at me. But it didn't matter to me at all since I was doubled over with laughter. I think their wild enthusiastic response about the possibility of us winning the lottery was guaranteed and expected from our money-based world, but it still was fascinating to me. I won nothing that night but I sure had a good laugh.

I guess on some level we'd all like to win the lottery. Why not? We'd have lots of money and could do almost anything we wanted to do. Right? Well, not exactly. First of all, wherever you win your jackpot, the state takes about thirty percent of your money for taxes before you see it. Let's not forget that. So if you won a million dollars, you already have it reduced to seven hundred thousand dollars in the blink of an eye. Don't get me wrong, though. I'll take the seven hundred thousand happily. And it's true that a large amount of money will give you a chance to do things you may never have been able to do before. But most people make a big mistake when they think of winning a lottery. They think the money will make them happy. The money will give them more flexibility to do things and to buy things. But sorry, the money will not guarantee happiness. Remember, in this country, we are given life and liberty, but we only get the pursuit of happiness. And happiness is not about how much money you have. Any rich person knows this fact oh so well and would tell you it's true—that is, if they were willing to admit it. But most wealthy people have a hard time copping to the truth about this fact. It's too humiliating for most of them to admit it because they don't want to be seen as troubled and struggling in spite of having money. That would expose them as having normal problems, just like the rest of us. That's their part of the myth about money, and it helps keep the game of chasing money alive. In addition, most people who don't have money would be very confused to learn that many rich people are not happy people. Those who work hard just to get by and pay their bills can't understand how you could have lots of money and not be happy, since so much of their lives are all about chasing money for the happiness they think it will bring them. It's a big bubble of illusion and nobody wants to bust the bubble.

Maybe our founding fathers should have kept our quest for happiness totally out of the motto. Maybe it would have been more realistic if it were "life, liberty, and the pursuit of money."

In 2005, I moved back to the New York area. Want to guess what I did? I started another lottery syndicate—this time, focused on the New York lottery. I reached out to a bunch of friends and acquaintances and collected fifty bucks from each of them and, once again, bought the new crowd of hopeful believers a six-month subscription. It was the very same deal as in Florida. But this group lasted for a year and a half with three six-month subscriptions. And, once again, I must report that we didn't win anything much. However, I think the reason we lasted that long was because I added something special to the syndicate. I hosted a meeting once a month for all members. We'd get together, share some food, and have what I called an abundance meeting. Each month, we talked about winning the lottery, what good we'd do with the money, which charities we'd donate to, and how the money would enhance our lives and the lives of our local community. We focused on bringing abundance into our lives and we refused any negative talk from any of the members. This turned out to be very special. Each month, all members looked forward to the abundance meetings. They were social and very uplifting, not just about the lottery but about all aspects of our individual lives. THINK ABUNDANT! We never won the lottery but I still believe that it's completely possible. Possible, yes. Probable, no. But I'll hold on to that belief almost as a quiet tribute to my father.

The group broke up after the eighteen months of play. After all, we got together to win the lottery and that goal was never met. But one member said it was well worth the fifty bucks every six months to be a part of such an inspiring group of people. So, in the end, it cost each of us about one hundred fifty bucks over the year and a half and in that period of time we developed meaningful friendships, some of which still remain. The loser mentality looks at that situation and says we lost. The winners look at the same scenario and say that we won. Which way do you see it?

CHAPTER 28

THE NEW WORLD OF SPORTS TALK

"Say what you feel. Those who mind don't matter and those who matter don't mind."

"I may not agree with your opinion at times, but I'll always defend your right to have it." Ida Klein

It took years for me to learn the subtleties and nuances to become a halfway decent gambler, but I grew up with a very natural and innocent love for sports as a kid. The best days ever were when a bunch of my friends would get together, head off in the morning to the Parade Grounds in Brooklyn, lay claim to one of the baseball fields, and play hardball or softball for hours. Going down to the local schoolyard and getting into a pick-up softball game or stickball game was really fun also. And usually after a day of playing some sport, football, baseball, basketball, or handball, we'd drag our exhausted bodies' home, have some dinner with our families, and get right back outside to play some more until it was just too dark to see the ball. At that point, we'd spend the rest of the night playing intense games of ping pong, or on quieter winter evenings a game of Monopoly, Risk, or Scrabble. We were into playing all the time and most of our play was focused around sports and competition. Nothing mattered except the game. When the game was over, we'd talk about the game, remembering the great plays and goofing on each other about any screw-ups or mishandled plays. And when we got tired of talking about the game we just played, well, we'd start talking about the next game that was coming up. We were all totally focused on the game and everything else took a backseat.

After losing my sight, I still had a strong desire to be involved in sports in some way other than gambling, so staying up-to-date with all the drama of the professional sports teams became a passion of mine. Years ago, I used to flip the TV on and watch the New York Mets. I loved being a Met fan, even though they weren't good in their early years. I was right there at the polo grounds for their inception with Casey Stengel and all of their one hundred twenty losses in 1962, and then I cheered them on all the way to the top with Tom Seaver, Jerry Koosman, and the 1969 championship season. My father hated the Yankees and although I quietly followed the Yanks and Mickey Mantle—one of my favorite players—over the years, I never felt comfortable openly rooting for them to do well; clearly a result of my father's influence on me.

I grew up religiously watching *ABC's Wide World of Sports*, college and professional football, the Olympics, and basically any sport that was on the tube. My world was sports and I was either watching it on TV or outside playing. The competition was always compelling and my desire to excel at sports was a driving factor, but, at the end of the day, it all boiled down to winning and losing—"the thrill of victory and the agony of defeat."

As the years passed, I slowly shifted from listening to sports on TV to listening to the radio. The sports announcers on the radio were much more creative with their play-by-play descriptions. They had to be. It was their job to paint a picture for those listeners who couldn't see the game. The TV announcers got to be more laid-back knowing that their audience could see all that was happening. So I obviously made the switch to radio and continue to enjoy it to this day. I grew up with enjoying announcers like Bob Murphy, Ralph Kiner, and Lindsay Nelson for the Mets, and Mel Allen, Red Barber, and Phil Rizzuto for the Yankees. And, today, my favorites are Howie Rose for the Mets, and, of course, John Sterling for the Yanks.

About twenty-five years ago, give or take a year or two, the sports world implemented a big change. Sports talk radio was the new experiment, and as you all probably know, it was a major hit, and still is incredibly successful. I really enjoyed listening to the *Mike and the Mad Dog* show in the afternoons on The Fan, WFAN in New York. The show consisted of constantly updated sports news, interviews with sports celebrities, stimulating banter between the two hosts, and questions and comments from listeners who would call in to talk on the air. In many ways, this new sports talk show was doing the same thing we all did naturally as kids many years ago—talking about the game. The show was lots of fun, informative, provocative with healthy controversy, a must listen to. To this day, I check the time when I am home to see if I can catch Mike Francesa's opening monologue, which comes on right after the 1:00 PM sports update. I've been listening to the Fan for over twenty-five years now and I still love it. In some way, it feels like a connection to my childhood and growing up in Brooklyn.

A few years ago, the FAN started a new segment. On *Football Friday*, as it is promoted, the Fan's radio jocks give out their football picks for the upcoming weekend. The station is obligated to add the disclaimer that they do not encourage gambling, but everybody knows why the Friday shows are so popular. All the listeners want to know which teams are picked to win by their favorite jock hosts, and maybe you can make some good money betting on who they like. Sports and gambling have always been married to each other, whether traditional sports enthusiasts want to admit it or not. Ever since I remember, people were always betting on which team was going to win, which boxer was going to knock out the other guy, or which horse was going to be the fastest in the land. I still remember when Cassius Clay (Muhammad Ali) upset Sonny Liston for the heavyweight championship. The fight took place over fifty years ago, yet I still remember that Clay was seven to one in the betting odds and everybody I knew back then was totally focused on the fight. People love to gamble and people love to watch sports, hence the obvious marriage.

It's amusing to see how much time and energy is spent by others including myself who are listening closely to the radio with the hopes of getting some hot information that will help them decide who to bet in the next game. We all are hoping for what we'd like to believe is an opportunity to make an informed bet on some team and then happily reap the rewards when that team succeeds. When we win a bet, we collect some money which is always nice, but we also get a moment to feel smart, the bragging rights, and that feeling for some of us may actually be more important than the cash. That's the essence of the game, to continually chase the carrot with the belief that you can, and hopefully will clean up more often than not.

Unfortunately, it doesn't always work out that way as we all know. When you're hot you're hot, and when you're not you're not, in spite of all that "inside" information ... and that's just the way it goes. I smile and get a warm feeling throughout my body every time I think of all of my past winning streaks, but I must have had at least as many losing streaks in my past. Funny how I just can't seem to remember many of them. Well ... once again, let's be honest here. I know they happened and they were all pretty painful, but I always seem to avoid thinking about them. It's that wonderful part of our brain that helps us forget the painful past.

Some of the past is worth forgetting, but some past experiences I've had in the gambling world were simply mind-boggling in spite of the pain, and I'll never forget them. I used to go down to Flagler dog track in Miami to gamble on the dogs. It was just another way to pass the time with my friends while trying to increase my bankroll. As most smart gamblers know, good luck comes and good luck goes. You just need to know when to put the hammer down and when to lighten up. I know friends who bet on horses that broke down on the track and had to be put down on the spot. That's pretty sad and incredibly painful to watch, especially if you bet on the unlucky horse.

But I once made the unfortunate bet on a dog that actually jumped the fence during a race, and the authorities had to catch him wandering around in the track parking lot. That was bad luck, but simply astonishing. I also remember a dog that, because of an electrical glitch in the equipment, actually caught the "rabbit" that he was trained to chase. Well, the dog never showed an interest in chasing the rabbit again. Interesting, huh! No matter what they tried, the trainers could no longer trick the dog into running after the elusive "rabbit," the electrical apparatus. The gig was up. That dog became totally useless as a racer. Is there a lesson in there for us? Have we been trained just like the dogs? What is the carrot we have all been conditioned to chase, and what would we do if we succeeded in catching that carrot? Would the game still hold the same interest for us, or would we just find another game to be an outlet for our desire to take risks? I honestly don't know.

Recently, I've become intrigued with an observation about the kind of conversations that tend to dominate the sports talk shows. Usually, the interviews are interesting and filled with insights about the celebrity's sport as well as the human side of sports that we often don't hear about. That's all good stuff. But after listening to many hours of sports talk radio for over twenty years, I've noticed—or should I say that it appears to me—that currently, a majority of the listeners who call in just want to complain over and over again about one thing or another. If the player hit two home runs, the callers often want to point out that he should have had three homers. If the team won twelve to six, the callers want to focus more on the poor pitching because they gave up six runs rather than the good hitting that helped the team win the game.

To top it off, like icing on the cake, it appears that the sports talk hosts, whether quietly nudged by upper management's guiding hand or not, may at times actually be more encouraging toward the negative. Controversy and criticism of sports teams and players may actually receive higher ratings and may be viewed as more interesting radio. In fact, when R.A. Dickey won the CY Young award in 2012, a prestigious award that only two other Met pitchers have ever won in their over fifty years of existence, he amazingly received such a small amount of airtime for such a wonderful accomplishment. The hosts and the callers were sincerely happy for him, but then, within such a short period of time, the attention of the callers as well as the hosts went right back toward all the things to complain about. Wow! Is this the underlying lure of sports talk radio? Is it to get a chance to complain with the whole world listening? Or to listen intently to those callers who are complaining about all the problems on their favorite team? And then to have a reaction to their moaning and groaning? Is it just an opportunity for those who call in to get a chance to vent about all the things that are pissing them off?

A large majority of callers are male and my guess is that most do not go to therapy for help. If this is true, then maybe the sports talk shows are unintentionally doing an incredible service to their listening communities by giving all those guys a chance to get some steam off their chests in a way that doesn't hurt anybody. Taking this idea further, it's possible that some men's lives and the lives of their families actually go a little better after the men get their chance to complain on the radio. Who needs therapy when you can just call up your local sports talk show and vent for a few minutes?

I know how it is for me. If I'm feeling lousy for one reason or another or I just lost a bet, I seek out somebody to listen to me whine and moan about the pain or the loss. It just feels a little better when I get a chance to vent. Five or ten minutes of moaning, and really, there's no other honest way to describe it, often is all I need to move on, but if I don't get those minutes, the lousy feeling from losing can stick to me like slimy goo for a much longer period of time. I prefer to seek out somebody who understands what I'm miserable about also. Birds of a feather flock together. But maybe it's more than that. Here's where the phrase, "Misery loves company" may fit nicely. If I'm going to complain, I definitely prefer a person listening who understands why I'm upset. Those who call in the sports talk shows know they have a large, sympathetic, informed audience who can relate. Even if there is widespread disagreement about a sports situation, the ensuing argument on the radio, which often can get quite heated, may very well have a subtle healing affect on all the listeners. I think it's ultimately a good thing, but others may see this as a little weird. How do you feel about it?

Anyway, as much as I love sports, I can see how in some strange way sports and the sports talk shows are our soap opera. Tune in tomorrow to find out the latest happenings on *As The Yankees Turn* or *Search For the Mets*. It's on every day and we, the listeners, get to play our parts in the daily dramatics. Some characters we listen to on the radio are really bizarre, some are happy, but more are not. There are too many commercials and we can't wait until the show comes on tomorrow because there's always more to talk about.

CHAPTER 29

LUCKY TOWN

Round and round she goes, where she stops nobody knows.

When I was around ten or eleven years old, my friend, Jerry, received a roulette game as a present. I was open to playing any new game, so I learned the rules and immediately immersed myself in the game. It was fun to spin the roulette wheel, drop the silver ball into the spinning wheel, and watch to see where the little ball would end up. Jerry and I would take turns being the house or the player, but after playing a while, the game became boring. The house almost always lost. I remember making bets on either black or red, combinations of numbers or individual numbers and, without fail, I would always win lots of money and break the bank. (Little did I know at the time that many years later, I would dream of having that kind of good fortune in roulette at the casinos.)

Many years passed before I played roulette again, this time on a cruise in the Caribbean in the late nineties. I was with Gretchen, my partner at that time. I could feel how much she wanted to support my desire to have fun, but really wasn't into gambling at all. I didn't seem to care. My desire was strong, so we decided to play.

I'd sit next to her and tell her which numbers to bet on. She was a little intimidated by the scene, a bunch of gamblers watching her every move while she received directions from her blind friend. In spite of the challenging atmosphere, though, I thought she was doing just fine. Then, at one point, we had ten bucks on a four-number combo and one of our numbers came in. She got excited and went to collect the winnings, when everybody, including the croupier, put their hands up and glared at her, stopping her cold in her tracks. She froze, appeared confused, and didn't move a muscle at that point. When the croupier pushed the winning chips toward us, she shyly took them but she was way too scared to reach over and take our original ten-dollar chip off the table. After biting my lip so I wouldn't burst out laughing, I was dumbstruck when we accidently won again on the very next spin of the wheel, as another one of our numbers from the same combo bet came in. Bata bing bata boom. Now, that's lucky! We won about two hundred dollars that first time. I gave her half the winnings, hoping she would become more interested in returning later to play again. I wonder how many friends reluctantly got involved with gambling simply because they wanted to support a partner's desire to play.

We did come back the next day, and sure enough we won again, about a hundred bucks that time. Unfortunately, though, throughout the evening at the table, she remained very cautious when placing bets down, never totally recovering from the incident of the day before. Still laughing quietly to myself, I gave her all the profits this time in my attempt to keep her happy. Well, if you want to gamble, you got to do what you got to do. Right?

The casino was using a big wheel this time and I didn't get to drop the silver ball, but winning at roulette felt very familiar. Just as I remembered it as a kid with my friend, Jerry, so many years before.

We went on another cruise a year later, this time in the Mediterranean. It seems like all cruises have little casinos these days and this cruise was no different. Being a nonsmoker, though, I didn't appreciate all the smokers and the smoke-filled room, so we only played a little. That time, I won a little and lost a little and came out about even. Honestly! But the gambling juice in my body was activated from the visit and the compass was now set on getting myself to a real casino. Enter Atlantic City!

It's actually hard to believe, with my whole life immersed in gambling, that I never set foot in a Las Vegas or Atlantic City casino until I was in my early sixties. I, however, did spend about an hour once in the casino in the Bahamas when one of the cruise ships stopped there for the day. It was an uneventful visit though. I went there more to honor an old memory than to do a lot of gambling. I remember slowly walking through the casino, feeling the energy in the place, then smiling when I thought of my friend, Jay, and his thrilling adventure in that very casino many years ago.

In the mid-sixties when I was attending the University of Miami, Jay, one of the guys who used to hang out at the poolroom, decided to take a short plane ride to Lucuya in the Bahamas to take a shot at the big money at the casino there. So we were hanging out in the poolroom the next day and one of the guys got a call from Jay. The message was to round up all the guys and be outside the student union at four in the afternoon for a surprise. Very cryptic, we all thought, but nevertheless we dutifully gathered outside at the designated time wondering what to expect. Then we saw this big black stretch limousine slowly pull up and Jay was in the car, smiling and waving to the guys. He slowly got out, looking very dapper in his sports jacket and clearly milking the moment for all its worth. Then he tipped the driver and the limousine pulled away. Next, he proudly turned to us, raised his hands in victory, and yelled out to us that he won two thousand bucks! We all gave him a standing ovation as we marched back into the poolroom. Jay was our hero for that moment in time. He stepped out, went big time, and conquered. A sweet memory of one of our own reaching the heights of royalty in our skewed picture of really making it—that is, as a successful gambler, of course.

The Borgata was my first stop in Atlantic City. Charlotte, my new partner, and I drove down with my excitement increasing as we got closer. Then Charlotte turned to me and, out of nowhere, told me she was a card-carrying member of the Borgata. Huh? You're what? Well, it's true that I had a life before I met her, so.... Next thing I know, we're at the Borgata and the place is jumping, the energy's electric, and I notice there is a part of me that feels like I died and went to gambling heaven.

A little more than a year has gone by since we walked into the Borgata. Since that beginning visit, we've also stayed at Bally's, Caesar's and Harrah's, and have visited Tropicana, Showboat, and the Taj Mahal. I learned a lot by watching my own behavior, as I initially mentioned in the introduction to this book, as well as observing many others immersed in gambling at all the different casinos. Here are some of the things I discovered.

SLOTS: I have no idea how many different kinds of slot machines there are, but I found out that each machine has a computer chip called an RNG chip. This Random Number Generator chip initially is programmed by the casino to pay back between eighty-five and ninety-seven percent of the money pumped into the slot machine over the long haul. So, in the long run, the house will always profit. For example, if we pump a million dollars into a machine over a period of time, that machine will give back about, let's say, nine hundred thousand. So, for every million that goes into the machine, we, the eager public, will get back about one hundred thousand dollars less. Some of us will win and many more of us will lose, and the house will take the profit of one hundred thousand bucks to the bank for every million pumped into that machine. That's the name of the game; however, anybody can walk in and hit a jackpot at any time. That's the seductive lure. And you don't have to have a working brain to win. It's pure luck. But it's also a real form of entertainment. Every now and then, and nobody knows when, the slot machine goes crazy and that's great fun for the lucky player who happens to be sitting in front of that machine at that time.

So charlotte's playing a slot machine and I'm sitting next to her. Nothing good is happening on my machine so I stop and watch her for a while. She looks at my sad face and asks me to try her machine. I'm reluctant, but decide to play just two dollars worth, win or lose. She happily gets up and, in the process of taking over her machine, I accidently bump into the Max button. The machine goes off and I hit a jackpot for one hundred fifty bucks. That's not just dumb luck. That's clumsy luck! She shrieked, I smiled sheepishly, then we both sat back with a growing excitement while the slot machine was making all kinds of cool noises and gyrations. Whether dumb or clumsy, a win is a win and I loved every bit of it. My body was starting to perspire as the bells and whistles kept going off and my face became flushed with heat. That wild rush of energy has some qualities that feel similar to orgasm, and I didn't even have to sneeze.

It appears to me that a majority of the people who are playing slots seem to be there for the entertainment of it all. They look, for the most part, to be a more relaxed group, almost accepting of losing as long as it's not too much. They also appear to be a friendlier bunch of people, many looking to strike up a light conversation with the person sitting next to them. Of course, there are others who just want to get totally involved in their specific slot machine and not be bothered by anybody. But, in general, I think the slot players are a more congenial, jovial bunch, their desire to be entertained just about equal to their desire to win. They are there to have fun, win or lose.

I think many from that same group feel more relaxed playing a machine on their own where they don't have to think too hard with people watching them at any one time. There's no one checking them out closely to see what kind of good or bad decisions they are making. The slots are safe. You can have your gambling experience without worrying about anybody judging you. Of course, you only then have to deal with your own inner judge, who I'm sure you know at times can be as brutal as anybody's. That's the bad news. But the good news is that you are the one who gets to set the programming in your head. You can be harsh on yourself or easy on yourself regardless of whether you win or lose.

Picture this: Our minds are just like a RNG chip with thousands of possible results from experiencing any spin of the wheel. Whatever happens outside your brain in the real world, you then get to have a reaction to it. It's just like any time you pull the handle on a slot and you hope for the best, and sometimes you win and sometimes you lose. The RNG chips in the casinos are programmed to give back less positive results and more negative results in the long run. Our brains are also programmed to react in positive or negative ways to external events. If you can learn to add a few more positive results when you pull your own handle, then you will be programmed to feel good more often and feel bad less often. Sounds reasonable? I think so. The most important thing to realize is that we are our own programmer. The casino's technicians have the power to change the settings so that their patrons can win back a higher or lower percentage of what gets pumped into the machines in the long run. But remember, the casinos will never program the slot machines to pay out more money than what they take in. They couldn't stay in business if they did that. However, we have the same power over our well being, but most of us are not aware of this power. It's simple, though. When you learn to feel good about yourself more and feel bad about yourself less, you have basically programmed yourself to be a winner.

A good place to experiment with this power is at the slot machines. Most people won't have the discipline or the desire to do this, but if you are willing, see if you can find a machine that you like and start playing. Try to take a minute or so to just notice what results cause what thoughts and feelings to arise for you. Then see if you can find a place where you had a negative reaction and see if you can soften your response so it doesn't feel so bad. A good one is if you play only three lines on a game and the fifth line would have given you some small jackpot. Can you do something nurturing to yourself instead of something to beat yourself up for not playing the max at that moment? When you beat yourself up or put yourself down, you are giving airtime to your inner loser. You can stay on that channel if you like self-abuse, or you can change the channel. Of course, if you missed a real big jackpot, all bets for reprogramming are off. It's a time to be pissed off and feel miserable. You have the right, at least for a few minutes.

I can't tell you how many times I was winning on a slot machine but kept playing until I pissed all my winnings away and ended up losing. The feeling I have after is consistent—I feel like a dummy. I know how hard it can be to walk away when you are ahead, but if you are winning at the slots, you are already bucking the odds. If you keep playing, anybody with half a brain knows that sooner or later you'll lose it all back and probably more in the long run. One healthy option is to leave when you're ahead, and cash in. Collect the money. Let it sit in your pocket for a while. Go for a walk. Get some fresh air. It's now your money. Doesn't it feel good? Take ownership of the money and enjoy those positive feelings. Of course, you feel like a winner. It's 'cause you just won some money. Isn't that the kind of feeling you want to get used to? Think about this. If every time you are ahead a good amount and you just keep playing, you are giving yourself a message that you are less comfortable walking away with the positive emotions and more comfortable with the negative ones. That's a loser message. I understand its part of the game to take a shot at hitting it big when you are already playing with house money. So take a shot ... every now and then. But see if you can walk away when you're ahead every now and then as well.

Another piece of useful information is that if you walk away from what you think is a "hot" machine, you struggle with the idea that you may be blowing it. Maybe another jackpot is right around the corner and I'm walking away? What am I, stupid? Not so! Actually, if ten different people sat down at that very same machine, they would get ten different results on the very next spin. According to the RNG chip information, there are hundreds of possible results based on microsecond changes. It's the digital age now and high tech chips that run the slots are lightning fast. If somebody pulls the lever and they hit a jackpot, it doesn't mean that you would have won that jackpot. The odds of that happening are extremely low because you would have had to pull that lever or press that spin button at the exact microsecond to get the same results. Remember this and next time it'll be a whole lot easier to walk away from that machine ... and hopefully with a nice chunk of change in your pocket!

Here's one more little tidbit to ruminate on: I've watched so many people including myself decide to play for just a few more minutes when it's about time to leave the casino. We play those few last minutes with a small amount of cash—five or ten dollars—with the fleeting hope that in those last few minutes, we'll hit a big jackpot.

"What the hell," we usually say, "it's only a few bucks!" Between you and me, I have NEVER EVER seen anybody win with their last few bucks. I have ALWAYS watched those last few dollars being sucked into the black hole of the slot machines, never to return. It's uncanny, almost like the machines have the ability to know that we're planning to leave real soon and we're playing with our last few bucks. Then it feels like they flip into a special program to make sure the slot gives back absolutely nothing under those conditions. I'm sure there's someone with a story of winning a nice jackpot on their last few dollars. But I have never seen it and it's never happened to me. So my thoughts are that it might be smarter to refuse the pull to play those few more minutes and keep the five or ten bucks in your pocket. Tomorrow is another day that we can gamble and it'll be here before you know it.

CHAPTER 30

CASINO PITFALLS

The key to life is to enjoy everything but be addicted to nothing.

"Know that I've forgotten precisely nothing; but I've driven it all out of my head for a time, even the memories—until I've radically improved my circumstances. Then ... then you'll see, I'll rise from the dead!" The Gambler, Dostoyevsky

The only person I am better than is the person I used to be. Wayne Dyer

It appears that the casinos in Atlantic City have been designed to have very different themes that will attract very different groups of people. This makes good sense from a business point of view, and based on the results, it surely looks like they've been quite successful. Do you have a favorite hotel to go to where the staff knows you and smiles when you show up? Lots of people have their favorite place and, for some, it almost feels like their home away from home.

I knew of a happy-go-lucky elderly man who enjoyed going to Atlantic City every week during his last few years of life. The staff knew him and enjoyed him almost as much as he enjoyed their friendship. He didn't win much. In fact, from what I heard, he lost pretty consistently. But he loved to go and be around the action and he looked forward each week to the day he would go to do a little gambling. The weekly ventures helped keep his mind sharp and his heart filled with the juice of life. He died at the ripe old age of ninety-three and some people thought he wasted his time and money during those last few years of life. It's true that with the money he lost, he probably could have helped feed a bunch of starving kids in some foreign country. But how old do you have to be before the judges of the world get off your back and just cheer you on, no matter what you choose to do with your last years? I look forward to those latter years of life myself and if I want to gamble, well, I'm going to gamble. Whether it's black jack, roulette, or slot machines, it'll be my choice. I don't care much about what the judges have to say. In fact, if the judges stopped judging everybody, maybe, just maybe, they could actually do some good in the world.

For total transparency, I must admit that years ago, I used to think that playing slot machines was about the dumbest thing a gambler could do. I had become a good gambler over the years because of my combined talent, intelligence, and guts, and playing the slot machines offered me absolutely no chance to exercise those abilities. However, something must have changed inside of me because, for some unknown reason, I actually can sit down and enjoy the slots every now and then. Go figure! Maybe it's because I don't have to do any intense thinking when playing the slots, and its sheer entertainment for me to see if the purest sense of Lady Luck is with me.

During one winter vacation, Charlotte and I visited a casino on Indian land in the South Florida area. We were looking forward to an entertaining evening of playing the slots and maybe a little table action with live black jack. We parked our car and innocently walked in to a very crowded, smoked-filled casino with the stimulating sounds of slot machines mixed with loud music blasting from big speakers. The energy was intense, intimidating to say the least, if not completely overwhelming to us. We were startled, but preceded stoically toward our goal of having a good time. I felt a tightness come over my body, and I noticed that Charlotte appeared to be immediately irritated and annoyed with me about who knows what. Not a good beginning to our evening.

We wandered aimlessly around the floor and through the crowded aisles for a while, awkwardly bumping into people on a regular basis, in our attempt to find two available slot machines next to each other. We enjoy sitting next to each other while playing slots so we can cheer each other on when either one of us hits something good and the bells and whistles of the slot go off. We finally found two machines next to each other and sat down to play. The machines were not of our choosing or liking, but once again, we trudged forward, put our member cards in the slots along with some cash, and began to play. There were some promotions offered that night, and one lure was to play for at least fifteen minutes on any one machine to make you eligible for one of the promotions. Although we had the best intention at heart, it was actually too painful for us to stay for a mere fifteen minutes under those conditions, in spite of the lure of the promotion. Of course, we lost on the machines. Wouldn't you have expected that under such duress? Anyway, we reluctantly decided to leave the casino. We marched to the door, looked back at the wild, chaotic scene, then turned back around and went through the door.

Once outside in the peace and quiet, and being able to breathe fresh air, we relaxed a little and thought about what had just happened. We started the evening with such a sweet anticipation of having a good time together, but the minute we walked into the casino, we both felt the unsettling energy. Different strokes for different folks. The place was packed and it looked like most people were having fun, but we were not. The reason we didn't immediately turn around and leave was simple: neither one of us wanted to disappoint the other. So we fought through our obvious negative physical reaction to the environment and focused on our desire to have a good time. Focusing on having a good time is a healthy point of view most of the time. But there are times that require us to honestly assess a situation and be flexible enough to change plans in the moment if it makes sense. Winners do this. We didn't initially do that and the result was not good. We came close to fighting with each other for no reason, just because our reaction to the energy of the place was taking us for a wild roller coaster ride that we were not in charge of. The good news is that we had enough sensitivity, thank heaven, to notice the very uncomfortable situation that obviously was not to our liking, and that we had enough sense to leave before too long. We got out just in the nick of time. If we had stayed much longer, we surely would have been at each other's throats and the inevitable mess could have taken a long time to repair. Attempting to force square pegs into round holes is a losing proposition.

I personally don't like breathing in air that's filled with cigarette smoke, but I don't begrudge the casinos on Indian land for allowing smoking. The state of Florida has a ban on smoking in all public buildings, so there is no smoking in all the other casinos. But the casinos on Indian land are not subject to Florida state laws. So those who are smokers have a casino they can attend with the option of lighting up if they choose. And now, those who do not smoke and prefer a smoke-free environment can go to the other casinos where smoking is prohibited. In some way, this works for all who love to gamble, whether you are a smoker or a nonsmoker.

But the underlying issue here is really not the environment. It's the feeling of disappointment—or should I say the constant attempt to avoid feeling disappointed, which is the real culprit. We gamblers know all too well the feeling of disappointment. The feeling of losing a photo in a horse race or having the dealer pull a twenty when we are sitting pretty with nineteen is an all too common experience for gamblers. The feeling sucks and there is no getting around it. We have no control over those tough breaks, and feeling pissed off or deeply disappointed seems appropriate.

The key is to make good decisions when we do have some control over a situation. If Charlotte and I immediately turned around and left the casino when we first got there, well, we would have stayed in a more positive mood. If we had stayed much longer than we did, we could have had a blow up and we both would have suffered. Its being in control of what we can be in control of, and then making healthy decisions that can make or break the mood, the evening, or even the relationship. I've said it before in this book and it's good to remember again that this is not the last chance we'll ever have to gamble. Tomorrow is another day and sometimes walking away in spite of our love of gambling is a winning decision.

CHAPTER 31

THE DARKER SIDE OF GAMBLING

"Who knows what evil lurks in the hearts of man? Only the Shadow knows for sure."

Every time Charlotte and I walk around the floor of a casino, there seems to be a distinct shift of energy from the area where the slot machines end and the table games begin. Games like black jack, Spanish black jack, and let it ride appear to attract people who seem to enjoy the social thing. They are quiet and thoughtful when they need to exercise some intelligence in their decision making, but also like to openly talk to others at the table. The roulette tables and the craps tables have a different energy. I'd say that roulette has more of a feminine feel to the flow of the game, whereas craps definitely has a strong male vibration.

And then there are the poker tables. It's quiet, intense, and very serious there. Here's where intelligence is needed, as well as a good working knowledge of the game. But even more than those qualities, the games of poker bring out the macho energy in the players. Here's where you find out if you have the guts or the balls or whatever you want to call it.

I used to love playing poker back in the days when I had sight. It was natural for me to pick up on all the "tells" from the other players. When one of the guys started looking around, I always raised with confidence against him, and when another guy started yawning, I quickly dropped out of the pot unless I had a full house or more. Those were the days my friend; ah, yes, and I made my share of decent money in poker. In some way, it's fortunate for me that I can't see now because if I could, well, let's just say I could easily turn into a casino degenerate. The temptation would be over the top for me.

I never played Texas Hold 'em, but it sure would be fun to give it a try. A friend who frequents casinos told me it's totally possible for me to sit at a table and play, of course with a sighted assistant, but I'm pretty sure I'd be too self-conscious about not being able to see the rest of the players at the table while they could check me out anytime they wanted to. Not good from my years of understanding the strategy of the game of poker. However, I've toyed with the idea of me and Charlotte or another friend as my sighted assistant playing Texas Hold'em on line. That way, I'm in the same boat with the other players—I can't see them and they can't see me. And then it's all about our cards, our smarts and our guts. The risk reward factor under those conditions would be intriguing for me. I look forward to giving it a shot someday.

Since I mentioned the internet, I'll share some of my thoughts about the online games. To be honest with you, I have a hard time totally trusting the integrity of the gambling web sites. Charlotte and I are pretty good black jack players—not the best, but halfway decent. We've gone online a number of times and played black jack and have yet to end any session ahead more than a few sheckles. Losing that consistently is almost as hard as winning consistently, as I stated in an earlier chapter. It boggles the odds. Logic dictates that we should win less than we lose, but we should win enough to keep us interested in playing more. That's the fun of gambling. You win every now and then and on occasion it's a nice win. Right? Well, at this point, I just don't trust those sites, at least as far as black jack and other interactive games are concerned where it's us against the house. So, from now on, I'm only going to put bets down on sports games or an occasional horse race. That way, I know they are basically playing the role of bookie rather than clandestine computer manipulators. Obviously, I have no idea if they are honest or not, but for me, I need to feel good about their integrity to put up my cash, and, at this time, I just don't. If you're going to play those online interactive games, I encourage you to be wary and remain thoughtful.

My paranoia regarding the possible lack of integrity that goes on within gambling institutions has run deep for me over the years. It's not new. I can't tell you how many times I heard, "Where there's a hungry horseman, I'll show you a horseman who is susceptible to some form of corruption." I read the Dick Francis books about horse racing and corruption and I'm sure those books had some influence on me. But I had some experiences, too. How many horse trainers and jockeys were caught with battery-operated buzzers, shocking the horse during a race to get the horse to go faster? I know for a fact that stuff has happened on occasion when the horse that finished last in his last four races all of a sudden wakes up and wins going away and pays ninety-five dollars to win on a two dollar bet.

I remember being at Roosevelt Raceway when I was in my late teens and I got to watch one of the drivers whip the horse with his right hand while holding the reins tight in his left hand. He appeared to be trying to win to the novice audience who only saw his right hand whipping the horse, but to the more astute, he sure looked like he was holding the horse back so another horse could win.

A bunch of my friends and I at Miami jai-alai picked up on what we thought was inside information. Maybe yes. Maybe no. But here's what happened: Right before a game would start, all the players would march out onto the court, turn and face the audience, raise their *cestas* in the air, and jog off to their waiting positions. Every now and then, this one player would jog out, raise his *cesta* in the air while looking out into the audience to maybe his sister or his mother or some friend and smile a certain way. When that smile appeared on his face, my friends and I would run to the windows to get a late bet in because that guy would almost always win when he'd show that particular smile. In fact, the guy would play like the best player in the world. Talk about a "tell"! We looked like crazy nuts running wildly to get those last minute bets in, but we made money way too often for it to have been sheer coincidence or pure luck.

When we went to the dog track, we'd watch for the dogs that just took a dump on the track because, obviously, they would be a little lighter and we thought hopefully a little faster. I don't remember winning much with that angle! But rumor had it that some of the trainers would inject their dogs at certain times with water to cause them to be bloated. Guess what? If the dog is carrying more water, he's not going to run as fast as he can. That's called fixing a race. I can't guarantee that this stuff happened, but you know the saying: "Where there's smoke, there's often fire."

My strong belief about corruption in the gambling world got so bad one year that I threw out the racing form entirely and just went to the track and watched the odds board. I'd watch for strange and abnormal changes in odds that would tell me that somebody who knew something special, or at least a lot more than I knew, just dumped a bunch of money on a horse. Or I'd bet the trainers who I thought were sneaky and would do anything to win.

At that point, I was driving myself crazy with unclean thoughts about all gambling institutions. I then knew I had to face something that was going to be very difficult for me. I realized I had only two options: to either make a decision to assume those gambling institutions were honest in general, or to make the decision to walk away completely from them and never look back. I knew I couldn't go on and keep gambling at those places with such a skewed, cynical point of view. So I did some soul searching, so to speak, and asked myself, "What actually is it that motivates me to gamble? Why do I want to keep gambling?"

I knew it wasn't just about winning money. I felt it was much deeper than that. So I backed off from all gambling and mulled this over for a few months until I was really ready to make a decision. At that point, I decided to trust the gambling institutions once again. I think it was a reasonable choice even though I couldn't prove to myself, beyond a shadow of a doubt, that everything was clean and legit. Despite that, I realized it would have been incredibly sad for me to give up this particular form of entertainment completely since it held such a nostalgic place in my life. So, today, whenever I go to gamble at a race track or jai-alai fronton, or casino for that matter, I stay focused on doing my best to enjoy myself, even though there's still a little voice inside my head that persists in urging me not to trust and to search for corrupt angles. But in spite of that little voice, I do my best to focus my attention on having fun and allowing myself to get totally immersed in a day of gambling. But now, after all that soul searching, I made one big change. I gave up the dream, or obsession, of hitting it big. After all those years of gambling with the belief, or should I say the hope, that I had a real shot at hitting it big, I decided to give up the idea of making that elusive fortune through gambling and to keep my focus on the fact that it is just a unique and deliciously engaging form of entertainment for me. I think, in my case, it's a healthier way to go.

CHAPTER 32

SYSTEM WISDOM?

"The only thing we need to decide is what to do with the time that is given to us." Gandalf

If you're a risk taker, then, somewhere in your past, you've probably dabbled in some system that you thought would help you be successful. Most gamblers I've known over the years have, at one time or another, indulged in trying to find a system that they could count on to help them win. I still catch myself every now and then doing this unconsciously, and then if something works for a while, it takes on a life of its own. Anytime I win on a slot machine, I inevitably want to go back to the same machine, hoping that it will be lucky for me again. Do you do that, too? And what about when you win at a black jack table? Don't you often go back to the very same table the next time you play? Some gamblers go even farther than that. They want to sit down at the same table and only play with the same dealer who was dealing when they won. They won with that dealer and they feel they will be lucky again with that dealer. All it takes is one good win to have the superstitious stuff bubble up. On a side note, I think it's interesting how the odds are consistently against you at a black jack table, and everyone knows that. No matter how much you are winning, no matter how hot you are, if you play long enough, you will almost certainly eventually lose. So why do most people feel the need to give a nice tip to the dealer after a good win? Superstition? Somehow, we bought the marketing piece that if we don't tip, we are destroying the good luck between ourselves and the dealer. Well, that's a bunch of hogwash. But if you believe it and then don't tip, well, you'll be conflicted in your head, and that's the worst thing you can do. Truth is the dealer is just a worker who is employed by the casino and probably doesn't make a great salary. So I'm sure they will always appreciate a nice tip. But, logically, they have absolutely no control over the way the cards get played out. If you tip them, I'm sure they'd like to see you win again. But it's just pure luck. However, it's interesting that in spite of the odds being against us, we are still driven to do what we have been conditioned to believe is "the right thing" whenever we get lucky enough to win: to give the dealer a percentage of our winnings. It's just something to think about.

Superstition runs wild among gamblers, but most people won't talk much about it. They'll just do some weird things if they think it will help them win. I knew a guy who would wear a specific shirt whenever he gambled. He was sure the shirt helped him in some way. Well, that shirt got pretty funky, but the guy kept wearing it whenever he went out to gamble. It was his good luck charm. Tons of people still carry a rabbit's foot or some lucky charm in their pockets to either help them win or help them ward off evil spirits. Yeah, gambling can bring out the superstitious stuff in the strangest ways. If you think it will help you win, you are going to do it, whatever it is. Sometimes, though, we attempt to use logic and we often create complex systems to help us reach the pearly gates of success, but I'll always take good luck over any system.

When I was about eighteen and just back from college for the summer, I combined my love of numbers with the horse racing past performances and came up with some interesting results. I was pretty new at the handicapping game and sincerely believed that I could find a winning system. I remember having long discussions with my friend's father who also was into handicapping the horses. He respected my intelligence and I'd get into explaining to him my latest system to win at the ponies. Since I had a captive audience, I got into lots of detail, explaining how I would add the horse's last three speed ratings together with a number for the track conditions on those days and the fractions the first two furlongs were run in. Then I'd subtract the weight of the jockey, the number of their post position, and the days between their last three races with some other horse racing minutia. After all those details, I'd come up with a final number for each horse, and the horse with the highest number was, according to my system, going to win. Although I never let on, it was amusing to me to watch this grown man be mesmerized by my every word, hoping to find the Holy Grail, a system that would consistently help him win at the races. Well, as you can probably guess, it didn't hold up. One week it would be good and the next week it would be horrible. So much for systems. And if you discover a system that always works, please contact me as soon as possible! I promise I won't tell anybody else.

A good system is really important when dealing with the gambling jones. All of us who love gambling know what it's like to get a gambling jones. It can sneak up on us out of the blue, and next thing you know, every thought is about gambling. It pulls at our attention, makes it very difficult for us to do our work, and it doesn't go away until we get the jones satisfied. It's no different from an ice cream craving, but the effects can be and often are much more intense than the sugar rush from ice cream. Our gambling muscles feel like they need a good workout. When you finally get a chance to satisfy that calling, you almost always feel more relaxed and sated, regardless if you win or lose. You know how that feels? AH! There's a deep sigh in your body and mind that can relax again. But the key here is to be the boss and to not allow the gambling jones to run the show.

Gamblers may be more connected to the planet than we think. The tides have cycles. The moon has cycles. The seasons are cyclical. We gamblers have cycles, too. For instance, every July, I used to get antsy for what I thought was no reason, until I remembered that the Saratoga racing meet was right around the corner. I would start feeling hungry for the action, and that hunger would grow until the horses began to run at the old race track.

So, if you get that gambling jones, try to understand that you are driving while under the influence; that is, of a powerful force. You can try to resist it or you can indulge in it. Both I think are destructive. What you resist persists. If you try to discipline yourself by starving yourself from the joys of gambling, you can and often will drive yourself crazy. It's like a diet or a fast. How many times do people attempt diets, only to eventually fail miserably and feel worse about themselves for failing? This is not a good approach.

Indulging obviously can often be destructive as well. How many times have friends or acquaintances that you knew lost control, got outrageous in their indulging in some way, and subsequently and unintentionally became destructive and hurt themselves or some loved ones? Indulging is not the way to go either. They are basically like two sides of the same coin.

So it's possible that you can come up with a specific system or a rhythm other than abstinence or indulgence to satisfy your particular form of gambling jones. Here are some tips that may help: First, do not try to eliminate it. Reducing it is possible; eliminating it is the kiss of death. A few people do have the discipline to completely eliminate it, but they are so few and far between that it's almost like hoping to hit a jackpot on a slot machine. Someone wins on occasion, but most people lose. The odds are stacked against you.

Another tip is to do your best to not feel bad about having a gambling jones. Face it head on. Accept that you love to gamble and work toward relaxing about it. Then sit down for a while and think about how you can train yourself to satisfy that feeling in a way that does not hurt yourself or any of your beloved friends and family. This is winner mentality. It's completely possible for you to do this and you are totally capable of setting boundaries for yourself. Thinking clearly is the key here. Too many gamblers check out with their thinking and just act on their intense emotions. This is not good. Danger Will Robinson! A cliff is approaching.

Thinking ahead is so much healthier. What system will work best for you? Tap into your creativity and I'm sure you'll find something just right for you. Here's one option of many possibilities: See if you can look at a calendar and set up a time to gamble. It's like making a date—not with a pretty woman, but with your gambling jones. And stick with your plan. Honestly assess whether once a month or once a week makes sense, and come up with a budget that you can honor. If you make friends with your gambling jones, you can enjoy yourself when those cycles arise, get your jones satisfied, and feel good about yourself. What a concept!

On a more somber note, I must bring up the long losing streak, a gambler's nightmare. Earlier in this book, I mentioned the trials and tribulations of losing streaks, but I talked about those situations with humor. Unfortunately, though, sometimes no matter what we do, we can't shift our negative perspective. We love to gamble and we want to gamble, but how many times can you go gambling and lose before you start going a little nuts? It happens when we get locked in a gambling rut, doing the same thing over and over again and getting the same bad results. I call this being hopelessly stuck. The only thing I know that occasionally works is to take a break from all gambling. It's a bitter pill to swallow if you love to gamble, but it may be the only thing that works to get you out of that hopelessly stuck place.

I remember getting into bad ruts when I played pool. I'd hit a wall for some unknown reason and everything I did would just turn to shit. I would get really down on myself, feeling totally lost and confused, but then grudgingly stop playing completely for a couple of weeks. When I'd pick up my cue stick again, I would be pleasantly surprised and honestly a little fascinated about how much better my game would be. I didn't do anything to make it better. I just stepped away from the game for a while. Sometimes taking a little space from the game that you love can make a world of difference.

Bitter is a taste that we know all too well as gamblers, and that taste can come in the strangest ways. Some people like to trust their subconscious to help them win. Sometimes it works. Sometimes it doesn't. I heard a funny story about some guy who used dreams as his method. Here's how it goes:

I knew a guy who had a dream about the number seven. He woke up smiling and noticed that it was July 7. Seven seven, he thought with a growing excitement. So he went downstairs, got the paper, and checked the horses that were running that day. Whoa! He couldn't believe his eyes. In the seventh race, a horse named Seven Stars was the number seven horse. So he ran down to his local off track betting parlor and bet seventy-seven dollars to win on the horse, and you're not going to believe what happened: the horse came in seventh!

Jory, my stepson, and I talk each week on the phone and every now and then we like to bet a few football games. Sometimes we win and sometimes we lose, but we always find reasons to laugh with each other, as well as at each other. Its fun, it's engaging, and it's a way to stay connected since I live on the East Coast and he lives out on the West Coast. We accidentally came up with a great system that is lots of fun and occasionally rewarding. After we make our regular, more serious bets, he asks me who I like in three other games. I tell him and then he bets a three-team parlay against all three teams that I chose. We laugh for a while and then he gives me three teams he likes in other games and I do the same, betting against all of his choices in a three-team parlay. We laugh a lot more and then wait for the games on Sunday to see if he gets bragging rights that week or if I get to goof on him for picking worse than a blind man.

If you have a system, I hope that it brings you at least as much fun as it brings you money. If you don't have a system, consider adopting the system I use with Jory. It's guaranteed to bring you and your son or your friends lots of entertainment and laughter ... and if your picks are really bad, it actually might make both of you some good money.

Looking back over my life as a gambler, it's been juicy and vibrant, wild and crazy at times, but constantly enriching and rewarding in many ways. My brain is sharp and in excellent shape as I roll past my sixty-fifth birthday, in part possibly thanks to my love of gambling and having so many decisions to make every time I place a wager. I wish I knew then what I know now, mostly about how to limit the self-abuse when I had gone through losing times. I mean, come on, who likes to lose? But now, after all these years, I know how to take a few minutes to allow myself to feel bad most of the time when I lose without feeling bad about myself. That's big. Winning and losing periods are like life cycles. They come and they go just like the night and the day. One almost always follows the other.

I have a distinct memory from years ago of watching Michael Jordan on national TV, with tears streaming down his face as he received the Most Valuable Player award in 1993. He had just won another basketball championship with the Chicago Bulls. And although it was his third basketball title in three years, this specific championship was extra special to Michael because it was only months ago that his father had been murdered.

Michael dedicated that year to his father, and now, having won the championship, appeared relieved, ecstatic, and filled with grief, all at the same time as he looked up to the sky with a wet face and yelled out, "I love you, Dad!" This was vintage Michael, a man's man, showing the world how to be open with the deep emotions of winning and losing, all at the same time. It was beautiful and amazing.

I sincerely wish all of you lots of gambling happiness in your future and a deeper understanding and acceptance of the times of tears.

CHAPTER 33

A WALK WITH CHARLIE

"Emancipate yourselves from mental slavery
None but ourselves can free our minds."
Redemption Song, Bob Marley

We all have had many teachers come and go in our lives. If we were fortunate, a few of them hold special places in our hearts and memories because they made a big difference, one way or another, in the way we saw the world and ourselves in it. Only a few had a good effect on me and my life, but I learned something from others, even though it wasn't necessarily all positive.

A very influential person in my life was Mrs. Morritt, my fifth grade teacher, but unfortunately for the wrong reasons. I never had warm feelings for Mrs. Morritt, and it appeared that she didn't particularly like me either. We had our little spats and confrontations, but, most of the time, they stayed minor. Until one time when I was so unruly, at least from her point of view, that, out of sheer frustration, she sent me home from school with a note that had to be signed by one of my parents before she would let me back in the class. In the note, she stated that, among other things, "Your son is a despicable young man...." I didn't know what "despicable" meant, but I sure learned quickly, and let me tell you, it isn't very pretty. Thanks to Mrs. Morritt, my rebellious, defiant behavior became legendary in my school, and it actually helped me feel a sense of pride in that part of my personality. After that incident, I was seen as a rebel, and I took to the image like a fish to water.

In high school, the most influential teacher I had was Mrs. Hendricks, a stern, intense geometry teacher who would get uptight at the drop of a hat. She didn't like the sound of clicking pens, so, every now and then, we'd get the whole class to click their pens at the same time. She'd go crazy, and we all loved the entertainment as a great distraction from the boring math she was trying to teach us. So, one day, I came home with my report card and grudgingly handed it over to my mother. She went over it carefully, then started laughing out loud with a strange look on her face. Mrs. Hendricks gave me a twenty in geometry for the first report of that semester. All my other marks were in the eighties and nineties. My mother shook her head in disbelief and said the teacher had to be crazy ... and she was. I ended up getting ninety-five on the Regents in geometry so I got to pass that course in spite of my crazy teacher. I think that class helped me understand the difference between my intelligence and my defiant behavior, but I also learned that I could use my intellect to figure my way out of any difficult situation.

When I lost my sight, my life obviously took a major turn. I really was lost and was desperately seeking some help. I luckily, and only by chance, got deeply involved in a counseling community that was focused on health and well being. The seventeen years I spent in that community was instrumental in helping me turn my life around and gave me the strength to build a wonderful life for myself in spite of my loss of vision. One of my teachers through all those years was Charlie, a big, strong, confident-looking blond man who had an amazing calm energy at his core. I attended three or four "Charlie Workshops" as they were called each year for all of the seventeen years of my involvement in that community. Charlie was one of my most important teachers, and what I learned from him was all good stuff. I left that community in 1996 and heard in 2006 that Charlie had passed away from a long battle with a terminal illness. I grieved when I heard the news, but felt so grateful that Charlie and I had had such a special connection over those past years.

One night, I woke up from a very intense dream that felt so real I expected to be soaked all over from having just jumped into a pond in my dream. I lay back in bed and was able to remember every detail of the dream. Here it is:

My dream: I was wandering aimlessly in the woods and I turned and saw a beautiful open meadow with a pond that looked so incredibly peaceful. Some guy was standing by the pond, smiling and waving to me. I looked closer and then I realized that it was Charlie. He kept smiling at me and waving. I perked up, stepped through the high grass and ambled over to him, but felt a little confused because I thought he was dead.

"Hey, Charlie, what are you doing here?" I blurted out, feeling that warm feeling I always got when I was around him. He looked at me for a moment, was just about to say something, then turned and pointed to the pond.

"I've been swimming here with the frogs. It's heaven. Healing waters. You ought to try it."

"I'd love to," I replied, "but maybe later. Want to go for a walk with me? I feel the need to keep moving my body."

Charlie glanced around, pointed to another path and got up. "Okay. Let's try that path."

We started walking with my left hand on his left shoulder like always, but I noticed that I could see just fine and didn't need to have him assist me. Before I could process that conundrum, Charlie spoke.

"So what's going on with you these days? How's life treating you?"

"Well, life is good in general, but I'm still so confused about my love of gambling. But how can I be here with you? Didn't you die a few years ago?"

Charlie burst into a deep belly laugh that seemed to echo in the woods. He then looked up to the sky and back to me and I could see a glow, a playful twinkle in his eyes. "You'll get it sooner or later," he said. We walked a little in silence, and then he spoke again.

"So what's the piece about gambling that you're struggling with?"

"Well, after all these years and all the counseling that I've done on healing myself, I still want to gamble. I know when I'm gambling at the casinos it's more than likely a losing proposition, but I still want to experience it. I just love something about being around the action. You know years ago when I didn't have a pot to piss in, gambling gave me a chance to get out of feeling poor and feeling bad about myself. But that was a long time ago and now I'm in good shape. I like who I am and I have financial security, but I still want to gamble."

I briefly glanced over to Charlie as we turned to our left on the path and began to climb up a small hill.

"Well, back then gambling gave you hope, a chance to develop your confidence in some skill and a connection to a social scene. Right? Didn't you have lots of friends from your gambling days?"

"Yeah. But that was then, and none of those guys ever turned out to be good trusted friends. When I started turning my life around, I lost those friends and made new ones, ones that I could trust a lot more."

"But it was still valuable for you at that time in your life. Didn't it help you with your confidence? Right? And now even though your life is grounded and much healthier than it was back then, still you may be just longing for something from that time. What do you think it is? The social connection? The feeling of being alive and excited about life? The competition?" Charlie stopped, bent down, and picked up a four leaf clover.

"You see this? Well, people for centuries have been searching for four leaf clovers because it's supposed to bring them good luck. Right? And, for thousands of years, people have been gambling just like they've been doing substances to alter their mind. It's inherent in the human condition to try something new, to take risks, and even to experiment with their bodies. Right?"

I took the four leaf clover, touched the tender tips, and slowly began to twirl it around in my fingers.

"Well, thanks to all those workshops you led, I was made to question everything about life, because there was so much ignorance and unhealthy behavior everywhere. I learned to watch my thoughts and feelings and to do my best to shift my life toward a healthier and more conscious direction. I worked hard and did exactly that and life is so much better now even without sight than it ever was when I had sight."

We started walking again as golden rays of sunlight came shining through the trees. Charlie laughed again with that deep resonating laugh, then started walking faster and began to speak again.

"Yeah. Weren't those workshops fun? Great stuff. The one thing you might have missed, though, was that I never said to give up the life you were living. You were running from feeling bad about yourself, so you felt the need to change your life and then you could feel better about yourself. I was just trying to give you the safety to face and

FEEL the guilt, the shame, the fear, and all that yukky stuff that none of us ever like to feel. That wasn't you. That was the crap you were carrying from all the ways you got hurt and confused as a kid."

We both stopped abruptly as a little chipmunk ran across the path right in front of us. Charlie continued.

"Remember when I told you at one of those workshops how happy I became when I finally cleaned up all the garbage I was carrying around for years, and then found my way back to my center? And how proud I was of that work? But that it was nothing less than hell to get through it all and that I was very happy and quite relieved because I knew I never had to go back to do that yukky work again?" Charlie shuddered and chuckled. "Yeah. I was glad I did it, but once was enough ... and I learned what I needed to learn."

I stared blankly at Charlie, still confused about what he meant. "So are you saying that I didn't have to change my external world? I just had to change my internal world? You mean the way I perceived myself and my life?"

"Sure," he said emphatically. "If you moved to Australia and you didn't do the work, well, then, all your internal garbage would eventually show up with you. You can't run from your internal world although many people try to, preferring to numb themselves to their inner lives with drugs and alcohol or some addictive behavior rather than taking the time to look at them. So are you getting this now? Do you get that this has nothing to do with gambling? It's not the gambling. Its how you feel about the gambling and how you feel about yourself because you love to gamble."

"So gambling is okay?"

"Sure!" he laughed. "Gambling is fine. It's just your way of taking risks, playing and competing. However, addiction is poison. Feeling bad about yourself is poison. Lashing out and hurting others is poison. Torturing yourself with all kinds of self-abuse is poison. But gambling's not poison."

I thought of the time I won the PICK 6 with Jory, won lots of money, and how great that felt. Then I flashed on losing so much money in the stock market and how bad that felt.

"So are you saying that it's not really about the winning or the losing? It's really about the good and bad feelings that I connect with winning and losing?" I briefly glanced over to Charlie as we slowed down a little. The sun was now directly behind him, and he appeared to glow again as his whole body was bathed in sunlight. "So do you think it's possible to lose and still feel good about yourself?"

Charlie burst into laughter again, turned to me, shrugged his shoulders, and took a breath.

"I don't know. Try it if you like. See what happens. But remember, you're running the show. You are the captain of your ship."

"And what if I get to the point where I'm always feeling good when I'm gambling? Why wouldn't I spend all my time in a casino, wasting my life away just feeling good?"

Charlie slowed down some more, smiled softly in my direction, and put his hand on my shoulder. It felt warm to the touch.

"Who knows what you're here to work on and to work through? But it's your life and you're really in charge of it whether you know it or not."

I was feeling wonderful, a rich warmth emanating throughout my body on this long walk in the woods with one of my favorite teachers. Just then, I looked up around the bend and I couldn't believe what I saw. It looked exactly like the meadow and pond where I first saw Charlie. We had walked far away from that pond, maybe a mile or two, or at least that's what I thought. I was confused and turned to him.

"Charlie, look. How could that be? Isn't that the same place where I first saw you? How could we possibly be right back from where we started?"

Charlie stopped, turned to me, and put both his strong hands on my shoulders. His piercing eyes probed deep into my eyes and I looked right back at him, feeling his love. For a moment, the world stopped and nothing mattered except our incredible connection. Then he spoke softly and with so much love for me.

"Marty, it's your dream. It's whatever you want it to be."

I felt Charlie's words go deep inside my being, then I slowly turned to look at the pond again and began to walk toward it. I felt a burning desire to jump in and feel my love of life and my love of nature. When I got to the pond's edge, I turned back to encourage Charlie to join me but he was gone. He just vanished into thin air. I was shaken for a moment but then I remembered his words. "It's your dream, Marty, and you're in charge." I took a big breath, stepped toward the pond, and jumped in.

EPILOGUE

"We don't stop playing because we grow old. We grow old because we stop playing." Henry David Thoreau

My father died at the age of eighty-three. During the last few years of his life, he enjoyed a daily drive to the mall where he would get his walk in and stop and have a cup of coffee and a Danish. That's all we knew about his ventures to the mall. It was a way to get out on his own and enjoy some exercise under safe and controlled conditions.

About four months after his death, my mother visited the same mall with a few of her friends. Out of nowhere, a big, rugged-looking black man wandered up to her and asked her if her husband was Harry Klein. Startled and initially taken aback by the man's appearance, she composed herself and slowly nodded with a confused smile. The man smiled back, pulled out eighty dollars from his pocket, and gently handed it to her. He timidly said, "I heard your husband passed away awhile ago. I'm sorry for your loss. He, uh, used to make some bets with me on the horses and, uh, he won his last bet." He then squeezed her hand softly and within a few seconds was gone.

When my mom told me about this, I realized that my father, in spite of his heart condition and his failing health, was determined enough to find himself a bookie so he could still have the juice that a bet on the horses provided for him. The money meant absolutely nothing to him at that point in his life, but the possibility of winning one more bet still gave him a rush.

I am my father's son, and even though we didn't get to enjoy the thrill of gambling together, I, just like him, still enjoy the juice of placing a bet and seeing if I can walk away a winner. I know that he would have died with a smile on his face if he knew his last bet was a winning one. Wouldn't you?

I hope you have enjoyed the wild swings from all the gambling adventures of my life. My wish is that a few of my insights become useful for you. Although it took me quite a while—actually years—to understand their significance, those insights have made a big difference to me. Remember, we who love to gamble, on some subtle level, are still seeking another replay of that deep connection to the primal adventure of life itself. We still get that familiar rush, swinging wildly with the unknown as we choose to play in the land of uncertainty. However, our fate does not lie in winning or losing at the game. Not really. That's the carrot we were trained to chase. Now, with a newfound awareness, we have a clear choice to understand that our fate lies in remembering we are the salt of the earth and that the big jackpot we have been seeking is not about dollars. Don't get me wrong. It wouldn't hurt to win a large amount of cash from some jackpot. That's true. But it's more about awakening to the miracle of what it means to be alive. We become real winners when we can honestly and humbly love ourselves for the person we've turned out to be. And this, my gambling friend, is what it's all about!